¡TOMA! MARGARITAS!

THE ORIGINAL GUIDE TO

MARGARITAS AND TEQUILA

By Robert Plotkin & Raymon Flores

BARMEDIA
1987

Dedications

To my Dad, Ray…who taught me how to get up in the morning
To my Mom, Carlotta…who taught me how to play the game
And to my mentor, Gil…who taught me to keep moving!

Raymon

To my sister — who ironically wouldn't know a margarita if it bit her on the knee—
Thank you for being such a marvelous big sister.
This is woefully inadequate, but you'll swat me if I say more. I love you.

Robert

Publishers:	Robert Plotkin, Carol Plotkin
Editors:	Carol Plotkin, Raymon Flores, Teresa Hermansen
Managing Editor:	Robert Plotkin
Production Manager:	Carol Plotkin
Cover Design:	Raymon Flores, Miguel Castillo, Maria Cecilia Boyed
Book Design:	Raymon Flores, Miguel Castillo
Photography:	Maria Cecilia Boyed, Eric Hinote
Additional Photography:	Sauza Image Library
Published by:	

BARMEDIA ◄1987►

BarMedia
P.O. Box 14486
Tucson, AZ 85732
520.747.8131
www.barmedia.com

Notice: The information in this book is true and correct to the best of our knowledge. It is offered with no guarantees on the part of the authors or BarMedia. The authors and publisher disclaim all liability in connection with the use of this book.

The publishers want to thank Domecq Importers and Sauza Tequila for allowing us the right to include on the back cover a picture of the magnificent mural by Gabriel Flores located in entry of La Perseverancia in Tequila.

Library of Congress Card Catalog Number:
ISBN: 0-945562-26-8

Printed in the U.S.A

CONTENTS

We're proud to have the support and endorsement
of these fine products.

Acknowledgements

We're proud of the association we have with our partners in this project. The companies we worked with assigned us marvelous professionals as their emissaries.

We are sincerely grateful for the participation of the people at Sauza, and particularly Mike Ginley, their national marketing director. His enthusiasm, vision and dedication proved enormously beneficial to this book.

The people at Remy Amerique, the importers of Cointreau ® Liqueur, (a product synonymous with the margarita), gave us the opportunity to work with Steve Kuhn. His considerable efforts on behalf of this project are greatly appreciated.

Last but not least, Mott's, importers of Rose's Lime Juice and Rose's Non-Alcoholic Triple Sec, not only gave us an opportunity to work with some outstanding folks, it caused us to become staunch fans of Rose's marketing director, Joanna Ebert.

We would like to express our appreciation to Carol Plotkin for her invaluable contributions as editor and project manager, and for being a constant source of inspiration. She deserves recognition for having to put up with both Ray and Robert. Without her ceaseless dedication, this book might still be a pile of cocktail napkins.

El Charro's David Guerrero, master mixologist and margarita guru, deserves our thanks and appreciation for his expertise and hard work. Any hesitancy on his part toward a drink would send us scrambling back to the drawing board;, a thumbs up and the margarita lived to see another day. We are proud to have included three sensational margaritas of his creation.

Our gratitude to Roger, Jason, Amanda and Bryan, the ¡Toma! Executive Tasting Team, for their constructive criticism and good humored cooperation. Thank you too for never letting us fully appreciate how distracting our shenanigans were to the smooth operation of the restaurant. Thanks also to Eric and Scotty, two exceptionally capable and professional bartenders, who more than tolerated our incessant experiments.

We greatly appreciate the participation of Carlotta Flores, author and culinary *tour de force*, for her endless encouragement and allowing us to publish her sumptuous recipes.

Producing a book is not an endeavor for the faint hearted. Carol, Ray and Robert are extremely grateful for the patience and contributions of three, highly skilled individuals. We want to first acknowledge Miguel Castillo, an artistic genius with both pen and keyboard, for his creative advice and tireless efforts on the cover and book design. If talent were bankable he'd be retired and living in the South of France.

We also want to extend our thanks to Maria Cecilia Boyed for her inspired cover photography. She listened to our ideas, applied her own vision and masterfully transformed them into photographic reality.

Thanks also to Eric Hinote, photographer extraordinaire, for his timely participation. His skill and expertise with a camera are evident throughout the book. He is a pleasure to work with.

And finally, our appreciation goes out to the esteemed and ebullient creator of "The Margarita," Margarita Sames, resident of San Antonio and citizen of the world. Without her, this book might well have been entitled, "Ray & Robert Knitting Across America." Enough said.

W hen we started this project, we knew the margarita was a popular cocktail, we just didn't fully realize exactly how popular it is. In 1969, an estimated 45 million margaritas were sold in the US. By 1992, that number had increased to 693 million with annual sales of $4.6 million. Five years later the number of margaritas sold in this country was estimated to have jumped almost 10% to 754 million.

Extrapolating the data we estimate the number of margaritas that will be sold in the United States in 2001 will be…well…huge.

Here's a cocktail that has defied the odds. The margarita has become an American success story despite not being from around these parts. Born and raised in Mexico, the margarita's personality reflects the flavor of its native land. Its fate has also been inextricably bound with tequila, a spirit that until recently was perceived as raw, raspy and suitable only for a shot glass. Not exactly the profile of a mainstream contender.

The margarita has nevertheless succeeded in the hotly contested American market. Its phenomenal popularity has made it the country's most frequently requested cocktail during warm weather, and second only to the martini when there's a chill in the air. More than just another pretty face in the crowd, the margarita is a bona fide, runaway success.

¡TOMA! MARGARITAS!

We first met in the spring of 1998 at Ray's restaurant, El Charro Cafe. It has been a featured attraction in Tucson since 1922, famous for serving the most extraordinary Mexican food found in the southwest. It was early into our first meeting that we discovered we shared at least two passions, tequila and margaritas.

That afternoon we went behind the bar and concocted more than a dozen specialty margaritas, each more savory than the one before. We played with different tequilas and tested various styles of presentation. By the time the salt had been wiped off the bar, we had decided to write a book. Since the lounge at El Charro is called ¡Toma!, which in Spanish means drink!, we decided to incorporate it into the title, ¡Toma! Margaritas! The Original Guide to Margaritas and Tequila.

Crammed inside these pages are 125 sensationally delicious, taste-tested margarita recipes, many of them our own creations, many submitted by mixologists and margarita maestros from around the world. And we did taste-test them all. We labored over the recipes for many months. When we thought we had one of the margaritas dead to rights, we sought the opinions of the ¡Toma! staff and guests, who tolerated our repeated requests to "try this one and tell us what you think." Rest assured, no laboratory animals were harmed during this process.

The heart and soul of the book may well be the chapter entitled, The Anatomy of the Margarita. In it we discuss every possible way to creatively tweak a margarita. Armed with this knowledge, there are no limits on what can be created.

At the risk of introducing a mercenary sounding concept, margaritas are also loaded with profit. Forgive us, but we've spent the better part of our lives serving the margarita-craving public, and we can't help recognizing a financial opportunity when we see one. It's a Pavlovian response thing. So to our fellow comrades in the hospitality industry, we're here to tell you there's gold in these drinks.

The other champion of this book is tequila. It has cast off its once lowly image to become the fastest growing spirit in the United States, increasing at a rate of about 3% a year. Without question, much of the category's popularity is due to the introduction of 100% blue agave tequilas into the American market. These ultra-premium tequilas rank among some of the finest spirits in the world, and have fostered legions of devotees. They are so rich and vibrant that you're left with the unmistakable conclusion that this is how tequila is meant to taste.

In closing, we urge you to take some time out of your hectic daily schedule to sip a margarita or two. It's a quality of life issue we're raising. A great margarita can make a bad haircut seem tolerable. We give you 125 great ways to smooth out the little day-to-day distractions. It's better than smelling the roses. Salud!

Robert Plotkin Raymon Flores

EL MUNDO DE TEQUILA

I t was a thirst for power and wealth that brought the Spanish Conquistadors to Mexico in 1521. In the name of the crown, they conquered Mexico and instituted a tyrannical regime, one bent on bleeding the land of its wealth and natural resources. The Spanish inexorably changed the face of Mexico, influencing, among other things, its language, architecture and social fabric.

The Spanish also brought with them the art and science of distillation, having themselves been introduced to distilling spirits in the eighth century. Arriving in Mexico, the Conquistadors found numerous Indian civilizations that made a fermented drink now known as pulque (pronounced 'pool-kay'). Made since shortly after the time of Christ, this viscous, milky drink is thought to be the oldest alcoholic beverage in North America.

Pulque is made from the fermented sap of the agave, a succulent related to the lily or aloe of which there are an estimated 500 varieties indigenous to the Mexico and Sonoran desert. The syrupy sap, known as aguamiel, ferments naturally and is low in alcohol. The Spanish, long used to the pleasures of wine and brandy, found pulque wanting, and took to distilling the fermented juice of several species of agave. These rudimentary, herbaceous spirits were called agave or mezcal wine.

In 1795, King Charles III of Spain granted the first license to the distillery owned by Jose Cuervo. What would eventually become Sauza's La Perseverancia distillery was founded and licensed in 1805. Numerous other distilleries began operation in the early 1800s. Distillers began cultivating agaves in large numbers.

Mexico set out on the long road to independence from Spain in 1810. Nearly 20 years later, General Santa Anna assumed control of the newly independent country, beginning a 55-year period of civil upheaval and military conflict. It was a dangerous time for the people of Mexico, including the numerous distillers of mezcal wine.

After a relatively brief period of governmental and economic stability, the country was again thrown into turmoil with the beginning of the Mexican Revolution in 1910. The following decade was marred by violence and hardship. A democratic government was finally instituted in May, 1920.

Tequila in its present form didn't appear on the scene until the latter nineteenth century, making it the youngest of the world's major spirits. In 1873, Don Cenobio Sauza began focusing on the singular properties of an indigenous variety of agave, the Agave tequilana Weber, or Weber blue agave. Situated in the small village of Tequila, Sauza started distilling his mezcal wine exclusively from blue agave. He dubbed the spirit *Vino Tequila*. Later that same year, Sauza became the first distiller to export his tequila, sending several barrels to the United States for an exposition.

Word of the special qualities of the Weber blue agave quickly spread to the other distillers situated in and around Tequila, and soon it became the standard.

THE MAKING OF TEQUILA

It could be said that Tequila was born out of the clash of tectonic plates and the volcanic cataclysms of the geologic ages.

The village of Tequila—meaning "hill of lava"—is very much the product of its volcanic past. Located some 40 miles northwest of Guadalajara in the state of Jalisco, the soil of Tequila is high in acid and silica, and the micro-climate is warm and dry. The dusty fields surrounding the village have historically fared poorly supporting conventional crops, with one notable exception—the local variety of agave, agave tequilanaWeber.

The adult Weber blue agave thrives in the rich volcanic soil of Tequila. At maturity, the majestic plant can reach a height of five to eight feet with a diameter spanning eight to twelve feet. The leaves, called *pencas*, of the blue agave are long, fleshy, and spear-shaped with sharp thorns on the tip and edges. The leaves have a silvery greenish blue color.

When the blue agave is between three and six years old, it produces rhizomes, underground stems that take root and grow into separate plants. Under cultivation, these small agave shoots, called *hijuelos*, are carefully unearthed and moved into a nursery. After a year, the young agaves are transplanted in the fields.

While every agave matures at its own pace, most reach maturity after 8 to 12 years. The agave must be harvested when the plant has reached its optimum maturity to ensure that the plant contains the highest amount of residual sugar.

The critical decision of when to harvest an agave is made by the *jimador* working in the fields. The *jimador* is a harvester, a highly sought after position requiring skill and considerable experience. An agave is deemed ready for harvesting several months after the plant produces its central flower stalk. The stalk is cut away, forcing the agave to concentrate its sugars in the plant's core. The *jimador* watches the plant closely, and when it begins to slightly shrink in size and rusty brown spots appear at the base, the agave is ready for harvesting.

Armed with a *coa*, a tool with an extremely sharp, half-moon shaped blade and a long handle, the *jimador* removes the agave from its roots and trims off the large, spiny leaves to expose the juice-swollen

core. With the leaves trimmed away, the agave's core resembles a pineapple, and thus it is referred to as a *piña*. The *piña* of a mature blue agave typically weighs between 110 and 198 pounds (50-90 kilos).

The piñas are loaded onto a truck and delivered to the distillery. There the *piñas* are split into quarters and then baked to convert the plant's natural starches into fermentable sugars. The traditional method of baking agaves is in a large stone oven called an *horno*. Steam is used to gradually raise the temperature inside the oven from between 135° to 145° Fahrenheit (F). It takes three days of roasting to fully convert the agaves' natural starches into fermentable sugars. This slow process ensures that the agaves are properly cooked and that the sugars don't caramelize.

The juice that secretes from the agaves during baking has an extremely high sugar content. This precious juice is referred to as the "first pressing." It is collected from a vent on the bottom of the oven and later added to the fermenting wash.

The softened baked agaves are removed from the oven and taken to the crusher. The machine shreds and mills the agaves, splitting open the plant's fibers and extracting the juice. Some distilleries still use a traditional *tohono* wheel—often weighing many tons—to crush the agaves to express the juice.

The extracted juice, called *aguamiel* or "honey water," is separated from the crushed fibers and transferred to a large fermentation tank. Water and yeast are added to the tank to start fermentation, a process that takes approximately 48-72 hours. During fermentation, the juice bubbles and boils as the sugars are slowly converted into ethyl alcohol and carbon dioxide.

When the fermentation process is complete, the fermented juice, called *mosto*, is transferred to the still. Most premium tequilas are distilled in traditional copper alembic stills. The size, volume and exact shape of the still plays a role in how the finished tequila will taste. Alembic stills vary in size from 250-liters to 3500-liters. It is thought that the smaller stills allow for greater quality assurance.

Once in the still, the *mosto* is heated to between 190°F and 205°F. The vaporization point of alcohol is 172.5°F. As the alcohol vapor rises in the still, it passes through a long neck at the top of the still and collects in the condenser coil. The coil is surrounded by a cuff of cold water which causes the alcohol to condense into a liquid.

This alcohol, referred to as *ordinario*, is transferred to a holding tank to await the second distillation. By law, tequila must be double distilled. For quality assurance, the alcohol obtained at the beginning and the end of the distillation, referred to as the "heads and tails," is discarded, or re-distilled in the next run.

The second distillation run turns the *ordinario* into tequila. When it leaves the still, the tequila is clear. Water is added to bring the alcohol content by volume to bottle proof, typically 80 proof (40% abv). It is again transferred into a holding tank, typically for 24 hours. At this point, some of the tequila is sent on to be aged in oak barrels, with the remainder being bottled as blanco or plata (silver) tequila.

The truest gauge of a tequila and the best way to assess its inherent attributes is to sample the blanco. Barrel-aging has a profound affect on tequila. Over time, wood imparts tannins that soften and mellow the tequila. Blancos, however, are bottled directly

from the still. They are vibrant, bursting with flavor, and best represent the wonderfully compelling qualities of tequila.

Blanco tequila is used to make *joven abocado*, or gold tequila. This is accomplished by adding caramel coloring and flavor additives to the tequila, giving it an amber/golden hue and a touch of sweetness or wood/oak flavor.

By law, Reposado (rested) tequila is aged in wood for a minimum of two months, although most remain in the wood four to eight months. Most reposado tequila are aged in large, wooden tanks known as *pipones*. The *pipones* range in capacity from 800-

liters to around 40,000-liters, with most coming in at 10,000-liters. The larger tanks allow the distiller to better control the level of woodiness in the tequila. Other distillers opt to age their reposado in 180-liter barrels. The smaller barrels impart more wood character to the tequila.

Reposado is the best selling style of tequila in Mexico. It is aged just long enough for its character to soften, while leaving the inherent quality of the agave unaffected by the tannins in the wood. A reposado tequila is delicate like a blanco, but with the added richness of wood. It strikes a true balance between the fresh, spirited character of a blanco tequila, and the mellow refinement of an añejo.

To be labeled an añejo tequila, the spirit must be aged a minimum of one year in barrels 600 liters or smaller, with most aged in 180-liter, oak barrels. The smaller barrels allow for greater quality control and impart more wood character to the tequila. The majority of distillers prefer to use barrels that have previously been used to age bourbon. Used barrels impart fewer tannins into the tequila and imbue the spirit with a subtle whiskey character.

Añejo tequilas are typically smooth and luxurious, with a subtle amber hue. They are characteristically aromatic with an exceptionally rich, well-rounded flavor, and a long, lingering finish. A well-crafted añejo tequila will achieve a nearly perfect balance of vanilla taken from the wood and spicy fruitiness derived from the agave.

NOT ALL TEQUILAS ARE CREATED EQUAL

Mixtos were the principle type of tequila imported into the United States until the 1960s. They are made from a blend containing a legal minimum of 60% agave and other, non-agave sugars. These sugars are added to the aguamiel and water mixture in the fermentation tank. Yeast is added and fermentation begins. Mixtos are typically distilled in technologically advanced column stills, much in the same manner as vodka. Column stills produce lighter bodied, more highly rectified spirits.

Because mixtos tequilas are made from blends, they are frequently inexpensive. Mixtos are also the only type of tequila that the government of Mexico allows to be exported in bulk and bottled outside of the country.

It is a mistake, however, to categorically dismiss *mixtos* as cheap and low quality. The best selling brands of tequila in the world are *mixtos*. Many brands of *mixto* tequila, especially the añejos, are a pleasure to drink. They are exuberant, lively spirits with an edgy, vibrant quality that distinguishes them from other spirits.

The premium counterpart to *mixto* tequilas are 100% agave tequilas. In Mexico, they are referred to as *tequila puro*. As the name would imply, these pure tequilas are made entirely out of blue agave, and typically contain no additives. The result is an exquisite spirit of incomparable quality. The production of 100% agave tequilas is closely scrutinized by the government to ensure exacting quality standards are maintained. The aging of both reposados and añejos is closely scrutinized. Seals are affixed to the opening of the barrels to certify when the tequila was barreled and to guarantee that nothing is added to the tequila as it ages. By law, a 100% blue agave tequila must state that fact on its front label.

The first sip of a 100% blue agave tequila will quickly reveal why it's the current craze. The rich character, taste, and aroma of the agave is remarkably appealing. These ultra-premium tequilas rank among some of the finest spirits in the world, and have fostered legions of devotees.

Premium, 100% agave tequilas are single-ingredient products. They essentially contain nothing but blue agave and a fractional amount of demineralized water. Contrary to some marketing campaigns, there are no closely held family recipes for *tequila puro* that are passed from one generation to the next.

Agave —
The common name for
the succulent plants related to the lily or
aloe found in Mexico and the American Southwest.

Agave Tequilana Weber — The variety of agave from which tequila is distilled.

Aguamiel — The unfermented sap of the agave.

Alembic Still — A type of still in which a fermented liquid is boiled and the resulting steam is condensed into alcohol.

Añejo — A tequila that has been aged a minimum of one year in barrels 600 liters or smaller, with most aged in 180-liter, oak barrels.

Autoclave — A stainless steel pressure cooker, varying in capacity, used by some distillers to bake the agave; replaces baking agaves in a traditional horno.

Bacanora — A distilled spirit made in Sonora from a variety of small agaves, the agave yaquiana.

Bagazo — The fibrous pulp of the agave remaining after the juice has been expressed.

Blanco — The name given to clear, unaged tequila. Also know as plata or silver.

DGN — Dirección General de Normas, the Mexican government's bureau responsible for certifying tequila standards.

Fábrica — The word for a tequila distillery.

Gold Tequila — see joven abocado

Horno — A large oven, typically constructed of stone and heated with steam, used to bake the agave.

Jimador — The person who harvests the agaves in the fields.

Joven Abocado — Also known as 'gold tequila,' joven abocado tequilas are unaged and contain caramel coloring and flavor additives, giving them an amber/golden hue and a touch of sweetness or wood/oak flavor.

Maguey — Another name for the agave.

Mezcal — A distilled spirit produced in Mexico. One significant difference between mezcal and tequila is that mezcal is made from the espadin agave (agave angustifolia haw) not the Weber blue agave. Also, mezcal is produced by cooking the agaves in covered pits or underground ovens, resulting in an extremely smoky spirit.

Mixto — A type of tequila made by blending up to 40% non-agave sugars with the agave aguamiel in the fermentation tank.

Mosto — The fermented juice of the agave prior to distillation.

NOM — "Norma Oficial Mexicana," a set of laws that establish standards of quality for the production of tequila. A NOM number is assigned to an individual distillery, signifying that the tequila was made by that distiller alone, and that the tequila passes all standards of quality. The four-digit NOM number appears on every label of tequila.

Ordinario — The term applied to the agave distillate resulting from the first distillation.

Piña — The core of the mature agave; named piña because of its close resemblance to a pineapple.

Pipones — Large, 10,000-liter wooden tanks used by distillers to age reposado tequila.

Plata — see blanco

Pulque — A milky drink, low in alcohol, made from the fermented sap of the agave. It is thought to be the oldest alcoholic beverage in North America.

Reposado — Meaning "rested," a reposado tequila must legally be aged in oak for a minimum of two months, but less than a year.

Silver Tequila — see blanco

Tequila — A distilled spirit produced within a restricted geographic zone of Mexico, double distilled from the fermented juice of the Weber blue agave (Agave Tequilana Weber).

Tequilero — A master distiller of tequila.

Don Cenobia Sauza is credited with a technological advancement that greatly improved the production process of tequila. Alembic stills of the day were heated over open fires. Exposure to the flames often resulted in scalding the *mosto* and badly scorching the copper bottom of the stills. Sauza rectified the problem by forcing live steam through coils located at the bottom of the still. The *mosto* heated evenly and without damaging the still. To this day alembic stills are heated using steam.

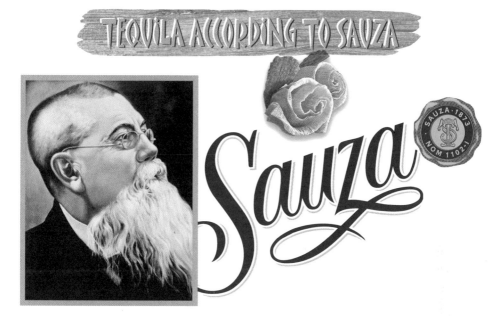

TEQUILA ACCORDING TO SAUZA

Sauza

equila in the mid-1800s was a small, remote village. Its dusty roads made transportation difficult, and communication with the outside world was virtually non-existent.

In 1858, a young Don Cenobio Sauza walked into the town of Tequila, and soon after began working in a mezcal wine fabrica, or distillery. At the time, there was no continuity of distilling, no standards to which the roughly ten local distillers conformed. Distribution consisted solely of selling their mezcal wine at a taberna, or cantina, located in the fabrica. Vino Tequila, as it was called, was little known outside of the immediate area.

Looking to establish a marketing advantage by expanding distribution, Sauza bought several stagecoaches and started selling mezcal wine throughout the state of Jalisco. Over the next several years, Sauza Vino Tequila was among the best known spirit in Mexico.

Don Cenobio Sauza is credited with being one of the leading innovators in the tequila industry. His most significant and far reaching contribution was identifying the distinctive qualities of a specific variety of agave now known as the Agave tequilana Weber, or Weber blue agave. He began distilling exclusively with the blue agave, convinced that it produced the finest mezcal wine. Other distillers took notice and soon the blue agave was the only variety used in Tequila to produce mezcal wine.

In 1873, Don Cenobio Sauza purchased an old distillery known as Antigua Cruz ("The Old Cross"). Later that same year, Sauza became the first distiller to export tequila to the United States. He sent a three barrel shipment to an international exposition being held in New Mexico. Sauza tequila was named best of the competition. It was the first of many awards earned at international expositions, which further propelled sales and advanced the reputation of Tequila Sauza.

By 1888, Tequila Sauza had distribution centers in Mazatlan, Mexico City, Monterey, and a concession in Spain. That same year, Don Cenobio renamed the family distillery La Perseverancia, saying that it was both in deference to the past and a pledge to honor the sanctity of tradition.

During the years leading up to the turn of the century, Tequila Sauza purchased fourteen other distilleries, this to expand production capabilities and to narrow the field of competitors. At the same time, Don Cenobio greatly increased the family's land holdings, devoting the fields to the cultivation of agave. The company was growing rapidly and now ranked among the largest producers of tequila.

When Don Cenobio Sauza died in 1906, directorship of the company was turned over to his son, Eladio, who proved to be a capable businessman. Continuing where his father left off, Don Eladio Sauza began a major renovation of the distillery and a modernization of its equipment. At the same time, he continued to expand distribution both domestically and abroad, and introduced new brands of Sauza tequila to meet the rapidly increasing demand.

With the advent of the 20th century, tequila as a category had emerged as a commodity on the world market. Mechanization greatly increased production, and bottling tequila widely broadened its sphere of influence. During the decade ending in 1910, the number of distilleries producing tequila grew from 68 to 87.

By the time Don Francisco Javier Sauza took over the company in 1931, worldwide demand for tequila was exceeding the industry's capability to produce it. In response, the distillers decided amongst themselves to permit the addition of non-agave sugars to supplement the aguamiel. Reducing the percentage of agave in tequila significantly expanded production. And mixto tequila was born.

Tequila was one of the few spirits whose supply was not disrupted by World War II. In 1945, a record one million gallons of tequila were exported to the United States. With the return to normalcy after the war, however, other major spirits were once again readily available. Spirits such as gin, rum, Scotch and brandy quickly returned to the popular forefront. The late '40s also saw the emergence of vodka as a mainstream liquor in the US. With interest dwindling, tequila nearly fell out of the market.

By 1948, worldwide consumption of tequila had dropped off dramatically. When exports to the United States and Europe all but stopped, it precipitated a wide spread financial crisis referred to as the "Tequila Crash." The majority of distillers slashed production, the others ceased operations altogether. Tequila Sauza's broad line of tequilas and international reputation greatly contributed to its survival.

The 1960s and '70s were good to the tequila industry, due largely to the spirit's resurgent popularity in the United States. While drinks such as the margarita, popper, and tequila sunrise contributed greatly to its growth, tequila principally clawed back into the US mainstream by way of the shot glass. The ritual lick of salt, squeeze of lime and toss the shot down the hatch became a familiar sight in bars around the country.

By the 1980s, tequila was a cultural icon. It appeared in movies, popular music, advertising and billboards. Rockers drank it on stage, celebrities called it by name. Tequila had really arrived. And so had Sauza.

THE TEQUILAS OF SAUZA

Tequila Sauza is today the second largest distiller of tequila, and the fastest growing spirit brand in the world. More meaningful to the people at Sauza, theirs is the best selling tequila in Mexico. To perpetuate its success, Tequila Sauza has over 80 million agaves under cultivation and over 2.1 million liters of añejo resting in oak barrels at any one time.

Under the watchful eye of master tequilero Oscar Duclaud, Sauza produces approximately 80,000 liters of tequila a day at La Perseverancia. The Sauza repertoire boasts of every type of tequila, each made according to the *"metodo tradititional,"* or the time-honored, traditional methods. As you'll see, a study of Sauza tequila is a study of tequila itself.

Sauza Blanco Tequila

Sauza has been distilling blanco tequila for more than a century, during which time it has grown to be the most popular brand of silver tequila in Mexico. Much of the credit for this fresh spirited tequila can be attributed to Sauza's singular production process.

Upon arriving on the truck from the fields, the agave piñas are off-loaded from the trucks and sent directly into the shredding machine, called a *desgarradora*. Milling the agaves prior to baking results in a more even extraction of sugar, which inevitably leads to a more flavorful tequila. Then prior to bottling, Sauza Blanco Tequila spends four months resting in stainless steel vats.

By their very nature, silver tequilas have a robust, exuberant character, and Sauza Blanco is no exception. It is a vibrant, unpretentious spirit, a popular favorite to drink as a shot or in a mixed drink. Sauza Blanco has a smooth texture and a spicy, peppery bouquet with floral and agave undertones. On the palate, the tequila is light and peppery with a touch of fruit in its finish. While not a complex tequila, the Blanco is well-structured with good agave flavor.

Sauza Blanco has earned numerous awards and honors, the most recent occurred in 1998 when it won a silver medal at the prestigious International Wine & Spirits Competition in London. It is an excellent tequila for use in margaritas because its feisty, assertive nature can easily be appreciated through the other ingredients.

Sauza Extra Gold Tequila

There is something wonderfully appealing about gold tequila, which is likely why it's the most popular type of tequila in America. It possesses almost every quality that one looks for in a traditional tequila, namely an assertive character, a lush, golden hue and a rich, agave and oak flavor.

Sauza Extra Gold is a *joven abocado* tequila. It comes out of the still as a blanco tequila and then rested in stainless steel vats for four months. Caramel coloring and flavorings are added to give it an amber/golden hue with a touch of sweetness and wood/oak flavor.

The Extra Gold has a rounder, smoother body than the blanco. It has a light, enticing earthy bouquet and a sweet palate of spice and oak. The finish is warm and restrained.

The Sauza Extra Gold is also an excellent candidate for use in margaritas, or any other cocktail for that matter. Its bold, aggressive character and fiery gold color make it an ideal base for a mixed drink.

Sauza Conmemorativo Añejo Tequila

Long before tequila became fashionable, the brand of choice of aficionados and connoisseurs alike was Sauza Conmemorativo Añejo. For many, this super-premium embodies all of the characteristics a great tequila should

possess. Being an extended-aged añejo, Conmemorativo has a smooth, delectable palate; being a *mixto* tequila, it's retained some feisty exuberance. This duality makes Conmemorativo Añejo an exquisite "must try" tequila.

The brand was introduced in 1968 to commemorate the unification of the 30 Mexican states. On the back of its front label are renderings of each of the thirty state flags surrounding the statue of the Angel of Mexico.

Unlike the vast majority of other *mixto* tequilas, Conmemorativo is aged long enough to be designated an añejo. In fact, it is aged longer than most 100% agave tequilas. Sauza ages Conmemorativo Añejo for two years in small, white American oak barrels called barricas de roble.

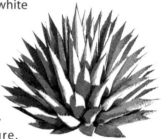

Sauza Conmemorativo Añejo is a classically structured tequila. It has a pale yellow hue and an expansive bouquet laced with the aromas of pepper, caramel, fruity agave and a hint of oak. In the mouth, the tequila has a full, rounded body and satiny texture. Conmemorativo's palate is a savory complex of semi-sweet flavors of vanilla, citrus and fruit with undertones of white pepper and toasty oak. It has a long, palate-warming finish.

While most purists would rightfully contend that Conmemorativo Añejo is best appreciated neat, those same purists would savor what the tequila contributes to a margarita. It blossoms in the cocktail, adding a seemingly endless array of flavors. So don't consider using Conmemorativo Añejo in a margarita as diluting a great tequila, think of it rather as an artistic stroke of genius.

Sauza Hornitos Reposado 100% Agave Tequila

Sauza struck pay dirt with the introduction of Hornitos Reposado, their first foray into the 100% agave tequila market. In Mexico, where reposado tequila is the spirit of choice, Hornitos has become one of the best selling brands. Equally significant, Sauza Hornitos has for years been the best selling reposado in the US, making it the company's most heavily exported 100% agave tequila.

Sauza ages Hornitos for four to six months in 39,800-liter oak vats called *tanques de roble*. The brand is so popular that Sauza has 3.5 million liters of Hornitos aging at any one point. These large wooden tanks are used because they impart less wood character to the tequila than if it were aged in smaller, 180-liter barrels.

Sauza Hornitos is ideally balanced. It is aged just long enough to soften its character without it being appreciably affected by the tannins in the wood. It has the exuberance and fresh agave character of a blanco tequila with a touch of mellow refinement of an añejo.

A quick sniff, sip and swallow will quickly reveal why Hornitos has become such a run-away success. The pale golden color belies its complexity and surprisingly full, rounded body. Hornitos has an alluring bouquet concentrated with the rich aromas of pepper, caramel and citrus. Its vibrant palate is an array of semisweet flavors, notably caramel, black pepper, luscious fruit and the herbaceous taste of agave. Hornitos finishes warm and long.

For all of its sophistication and market dominance, Sauza Hornitos is priced well below other 100% agave reposados, earning it the reputation as "the most tequila for the buck." It makes an excellent addition to any margarita, adding the distinctively earthy taste of a 100% agave tequila.

Sauza Galardon Gran Reposado
100% Agave Tequila

The word Galardon in English means the "highest prize," and in its own way, that is what Sauza Galardon Gran Reposado has achieved. Galardon is aged for eleven months, the maximum amount of time allowed by law. In fact, if it stayed in wood any longer it would be considered an añejo. No other reposado tequila equals it in age or elegance, earning Galardon the unofficial designation as a "Gran Reposado."

Introduced in 1997, Galardon Gran Reposado is the first of the ultra-premium 100% agave tequilas Sauza has teamed together as the Estate Collection. Extended aging is only one of Galardon's marks of distinction. The brand is also aged in small, 180-liter white oak barrels, rather than the large vats used to age Hornitos. The smaller barrels imbue Galardon with a more wooded personality.

The first indication that this reposado is genuinely something special is its bright amber hue and clean, satiny smooth texture. Its bouquet is compelling, a concentrated affair with notes of caramel, white pepper, toasted oak, and sweet spice. Galardon has a balanced, well-rounded body. Its complex palate is a tempting offering of sweet agave fruit, caramel, pepper and dry vegetal flavors. The protracted finish is warm and decidedly herbal.

Galardon has achieved preeminence as a reposado. In 1998, it earned a silver medal at the International Wine & Spirits Competition in London. The tequila is made in small batches and in limited quantity, which only serves to heighten its exclusivity. Sauza created for Galardon an intriguing, tooled metal label, conveying a heritage steeped in tradition and craftsmanship.

The unsurpassed qualities inherent in Galardon Gran Reposado are best appreciated when it is served neat, or in a slimmed down margarita that showcases the tequila.

Sauza Tres Generaciones Añejo 100% Agave Tequila

Sauza Tres Generaciones Añejo is a celebration of the lives of the company's founding fathers, Don Cenobio, Eladio and Francisco Javier Sauza, whose images are embossed into the readily identifiable, black-etched bottle. Popularly referred to as "Three Gs," this superlative añejo originated as a mixto, and has for years ranked among the super-premium elite. It is the second member of the Sauza Estate Collection.

The tequila is double-distilled in copper alembic stills and then aged a minimum of three years in 180-liter white oak barrels. In 1997, Sauza further added to the brand's popular appeal by debuting Tres Generaciones as a 100% agave añejo. The upgrade only served to further enhance this already outstanding tequila.

Tres Generaciones Añejo is an understated, sophisticated tequila. It has the pale, golden hue of white wine and a lush, seamlessly smooth body and texture. The tequila has an alluring, somewhat floral bouquet interlaced with the aromas of earthy agave, caramel and spice. Tres Generaciones is rich and supple, possessing a soft palate amply endowed with the flavors of citrus, pepper and toasted oak. The finish is long, warm and eminently satisfying.

In 1998, Tres Generaciones Añejo was awarded the coveted gold medal at the International Wine & Spirits Competition. It should come as no surprise that Tres Generaciones is at its finest when served neat so that it can properly oxygenate and be savored slowly. It is also outstanding in a margarita whose recipe allows it to take center stage.

Sauza Triada Añejo 100% Agave Tequila

The final member of the Estate Collection debuted in 1998, and after 140 years of making tequila, may be Sauza's finest achievement to-date. Heavyweight Sauza Triada 100% Agave Añejo is a super-premium tequila already being accorded top-shelf status.

This lavish, skillfully crafted tequila is double distilled from the first pressing of the agaves, the prime cut of the milling. Sauza Triada is also the product of a singular, two-stage aging process. It is first aged as a reposado in large oak vats. After roughly six months, the tequila is transferred to 180-liter, oak bourbon barrels. Prior to filling, the charred insides of the barrels are scraped away, leaving behind seasoned wood that imparts an intriguing spice to the tequila as it matures. Triada Añejo is left in the barrel for over three years.

Sauza Triada Añejo is flawless. It has a brilliant golden color and a magnificently full, rounded body. Its earthy bouquet is rich with the aromas of roasted agave, ripe fruit and toasted oak. Triada is exceptionally well balanced with a complex palate of oak, spice, almonds and fruit. Its finish is exceedingly long, warm and spicy.

While relatively new to the market, Sauza Triada Añejo is a guaranteed "can't miss."

There is a thin line between fact and fiction, a line that is often obscured with the passage of time. Such is the case surrounding the origin of the margarita, which occurred somewhere during a fifteen year span between the mid-1930s and the late '40s. Some versions of how the margarita originated cite the place of origin as the United States, others Mexico. Weeding through the conflicting accounts of how the drink originated quickly turned into a fascinating "who done it."

Most of the stories have been published in various newspaper and magazine articles. In each case, the author portrayed a particular version of the event, citing a sincere and seemingly credible source. Considering the extraordinary success of the cocktail, however, there is more than ample motivation for someone to claim he or she formulated the original margarita. Fame is a heady motivator. How then do we separate fact from fiction?

From the beginning, we presumed it was likely that more than one account of how the margarita originated could be true. For example, two different people working at two different bars may have each mixed together tequila, Cointreau® and lime juice and called it a margarita. The events could even be separated by a number of years. As a result, each person's claim as the cocktail's originator may seem to have legitimacy.

We've decided that for a person to have a legitimate claim as the originator of the margarita, a set of criteria must first be established. The credibility of a story weighs heavily on the credibility of its witnesses. It's a fact of life. When someone in the public eye, for instance a movie star or hotel tycoon, talks about a cocktail, people take notice and things start to happen. Soon bars from Manhattan to Manhattan Beach are serving the drink. That is how a cocktail becomes part of the American lexicon.

Second, the time frame of the margarita's origin is important. We are more inclined to believe an account that is said to have taken place in the 1940s than one occurring in the '30s. The recipe for the margarita can't be found in most drink guides until the mid 1950s.

Last, for an account to be afforded legitimacy as the origin of the margarita, its creation must have started a chain of events. Simply creating the drink and calling it a margarita is insufficient.

As for "who done it", we've looked at the evidence and have reached a verdict. Let's see if you agree.

THE CAST OF CHARACTERS

• Margarita Sames

San Antonio native Margarita Sames was a self-described socialite who, along with her husband Bill, owned a villa near the Flamingo Hotel in Acapulco, Mexico. The year was 1948 and times were good. The war had ended three years before and the country was experiencing a prolonged period of prosperity. For the rich and famous, Acapulco was an irresistible playground.

The Sames lived in Acapulco for part of the year. There they developed a close circle of friends, affectionately dubbed the "team." The cadre consisted of Fred MacMurray, Lana Turner, Nick Hilton, next door neighbor John Wayne, Joseph Drown, owner of the Hotel Bel-Air, and restaurateur Shelton McHenrie, owner of the Tail o' the Cock restaurant in Los Angeles.

This group of influential, high-profile friends was practically inseparable. They reveled in the festive, laid back attitude of Acapulco, spending their nights playing by the pool and downing a considerable number of cocktails. Lunch time was typically served somewhere around sunset.

Margarita Sames had an effervescent personality and disarming smile. She was a social magnet and the unofficial leader of the group. The Sames house was the setting for many wild parties, raucous affairs that sometimes lasted days on end.

Shortly before Christmas '48, Margarita Sames was challenged by several ranking members of the team to devise a new and exciting cocktail, something to break up their regimen of beer and Bloody Marys. Her initial attempts were loudly and unanimously rejected. After each round of successively worse drinks, her friends, this band of movie stars and distinguished businessmen, expressed their displeasure by tossing her in the pool.

Undaunted, a soaking wet Margarita Sames went back to work. She mixed together tequila and Cointreau with fresh lime juice. Having grown up in France, Sames was well-familiar with Cointreau, and after spending years vacationing in Mexico, she had developed an appreciation for Mexico's native spirit, tequila.

She tried several different formulations, however, some came out too sweet, some not sweet enough. Then she hit on what she thought was the perfect blend — one part Cointreau, three parts tequila and one part lime juice. Knowing that most people drank tequila preceded by a lick of salt, she chose to garnish her cocktail with a rim of course salt.

She brought out a tray of champagne glasses brimming with her new creation. Her friends sipped heartily and the approval was overwhelming. They proclaimed it a triumph. It quickly became the group's signature cocktail, the main course and featured attraction during Christmas and New Year's Eve.

Sames credits the proliferation of the drink to her friends, John Wayne, Fred MacMurray and Lana Turner. Her emissaries would go to restaurants and bars, tell the bartenders about the Margarita and order a few rounds. Soon it was a specialty at the Acapulco Airport. Nicky Hilton began promoting the cocktail at the bars in the popular Acapulco Hilton, as did Joe Drown at the Hotel Bel-Aire.

One account has the margarita originating at the fashionable Tail o' the Cock restaurant near Los Angeles. Owned by team member and Acapulco veteran Shelton McHenrie, the Tail o' the Cock restaurant may likely have been where many Americans first sampled Margarita's drink.

In the years following, Margarita Sames remained a socialite in the international set. She continued serving her cocktail to her growing host of friends. She spent many afternoons sipping margaritas with Eleanor Roosevelt, and the legendary baseball manager John McGraw was a lifelong friend of the Sames and the Margarita.

In 1993, her friends threw Margarita Sames an 82nd birthday party that lasted five days. The drink of choice...well, you can just imagine.

• Carlos Herrera

In the mid to late 1930s, many Americans would make their escape by driving across the border to dine and cavort at Rancho La Gloria, a popular restaurant & lounge located at Rosarita Beach, just south of Tijuana. The restaurant opened in 1935 and was owned and operated by Carlos Herrera. Rancho La Gloria was a favorite haunt of actor/musician Phil Harris, singer Alice Faye and their Hollywood friends.

One of the regulars at Rancho La Gloria was showgirl and part-time actress Marjorie King. As the story goes, she was allergic to alcohol, except for tequila, a spirit she unfortunately disliked. Carlos ventured behind the bar and decided to mix a jigger of tequila with lemon juice and Cointreau®. He served the cocktail in a glass rimmed with salt. She adored the drink and Herrera named the concoction in her honor, the Margarita.

The drink thrived at Rancho La Gloria and solidified Herrera's place in local history as the originator of Mexico's most famous cocktail. Carlos Herrera died in 1992 at the age of 90.

• Francisco "Pancho" Morales

In July 1942, Pancho Morales was a bartender at Tommy's Place, an El Paso tavern located near Fort Bliss, Texas. One day a woman sauntered into this popular G.I. bar and ordered a drink named the magnolia. According to the story, Morales knew only that the magnolia contained Cointreau® and could not recall the recipe's other ingredients. So, like any great bartender, he improvised.

Morales added tequila and lime juice to the Cointreau. The woman knew immediately the concoction was no magnolia, but found the cocktail superb nonetheless. When asked to name his increasingly popular specialty, Morales stuck with the floral-theme and dubbed the cocktail, the "Daisy," which in Spanish translates to the "Margarita."

• Danny Negrete

In 1936, Danny Negrete was the manager of the Garci Crespo Hotel, in Puebla, Mexico. Danny's girlfriend was a beautiful woman named Margarita. Her favorite drink consisted of a lick of table salt, a shot of tequila, and a squeeze of fresh lime. She was, however, self-conscious about dipping her fingers into the table salt bowl.

One night Negrete concocted a special drink for his girlfriend, one that would alleviate the need for her to continually dip her fingers in salt. He mixed tequila, Cointreau® and lime juice, and naturally served the drink with a rim of salt. She loved the drink, as did the others. Negrete suggests the rest is history.

• Johnny Durlesser and Vernon Underwood

During the mid-50s, few restaurants in the greater Los Angeles area were more popular than the Tail o' the Cock located on La Cienega Boulevard in the midst of restaurant row. The restaurant's lounge was nearly always jammed with the well-to-do and Hollywood luminaries. The bartending staff was top-notch and capably lead by head bartender Johnny Durlesser.

Vernon Underwood was the president of Young's Market Company, a liquor distributorship. The company had successfully negotiated for the rights to distribute Jose Cuervo tequila. Sometime in 1955, Underwood was shocked to learn that the Tail o' the Cock Restaurant was ordering on average five cases of the tequila per week. Tequila was still a fledgling spirit in the United States at the time, so ordering five cases a week was an unheard of. Underwood decided to investigate personally.

What he found was Durlesser had concocted a special drink for a lovely starlet named Margarita. The drink was made with tequila, Cointreau® and lime juice served in a cocktail glass rimmed with salt. The Margarita, as it was called, was an immediate success.

Underwood seized the opportunity and began running full-page advertisements in national magazines featuring a portrait of the woman with the slogan, "Margarita, more than a girl's name."

"Your Honor, We The Jury Find..."

To be fair, there are those who contend that the margarita is simply an evolutionary variation of the classic cocktail, the side car. Their contention is based on the fact that the side car preceded the margarita, and that the two recipes are strikingly similar.

The side car was created at Harry's New York Bar in Paris during World War I. It is made with cognac, Cointreau®, and lemon juice, then shaken with ice and served straight-up in a chilled cocktail glass rimmed with sugar. Substitute the cognac with tequila, the lemon juice for lime juice, replace the rim of sugar with salt and you've got a margarita.

So which story is true? Each sounds plausible, certainly credible enough for cocktail party conversation. Proof in this case is nearly non-existent, the evidence largely hearsay. Selecting just one of these stories as the bona fide account of how the margarita originated is challenging and certainly open for debate. This is not, however, an exercise for the faint hearted. History demands a decision.

We believe the strongest case can be made for Margarita Sames. At the onset, we said our litmus test of legitimacy consisted of three criteria, and the Margarita Sames' narrative more than meets these measures of legitimacy.

The drink's inauguration was well-attended by highly credible, highly influential people. The event is said to have taken place in December 1948, which is the time frame we're looking for. More important, Sames' creation started a chain of events that likely fueled the margarita's colonization.

Then there's the link between Margarita Sames and Tail o' the Cock owner Shelton McHenrie. The restaurant is often credited with being the birthplace of the margarita. It's plausible that McHenrie told Johnny Durlesser about the margarita, who may have over time embellished or reformulated the recipe and called it his own.

The last piece of circumstantial evidence is Margarita Sames French background. Cointreau® is considered a French national

treasure, found in nearly every household. Sames would naturally be familiar with Cointreau® and have a bottle on-hand. We weren't so inclined to believe the Cointreau®-connection with some of the other stories.

We did find the Carlos Herrera story convincing. There's every reason to believe that a drink made with tequila, Cointreau® and lime juice, named the margarita was a specialty of the house at the Rancho La Gloria restaurant during the late 1930s. Other than the word of mouth, however, there's no evidence suggesting how the Herrera concoction sparked an international migration.

Based on the information at-hand,
we find for Margarita Sames.

o what exactly is a margarita? Ask a hundred bartenders and you may well get 100 different answers. Sure they'd say that it contains tequila, triple sec and sweet 'n' sour. But how much of each ingredient? What are the proportions? What kind of sweet 'n' sour do you use—lime or lemon? The truth is that despite the margarita's enormous popularity there is no consensus as to its recipe.

Perhaps that's the way it should be. Creative latitude is a hallmark of the bar business. This same latitude swings both ways however, likely resulting in good people being served some fairly lame margaritas. We say enough! Enough guessing as to what makes a great margarita. Stop experimenting on friends and patrons like guinea pigs. It's time to set the record straight.

We offer the following margarita recipe for your consideration as a marvelous starting point. It's delicious and well-balanced. The recipe contains just enough tequila so you can taste it, but not so much that the tequila is overbearing. The margarita also features a number of subtle tastes that add dimension and enhance the drink's flavor profile. It can be served with pride to your guests and makes an excellent "house" margarita for a bar or restaurant.

THE MARGARITA

Cocktail or house specialty glass, chilled
(Salted rim and ice optional)
1 1/4 oz. Silver Tequila
1/2 oz. Triple Sec
1/2 oz. Rose's Lime Juice
(1/4 oz. orange juice optional)
1 1/2 oz. sweet 'n' sour mix
Shake and strain
Fresh lime wedge garnish

Alright then, there it is, our recommended margarita recipe. Why is this the recipe for the margarita? It's a valid question. Here's our answer, detailed ingredient by ingredient.

• Cocktail or house specialty glass, chilled

The margarita originated as a cocktail, and to this day serving the drink straight-up is the classic presentation. To prepare the drink, the ingredients are mixed in an iced shaker set and strained into a chilled, 4-6 ounce cocktail glass. Because the margarita is only briefly in contact with ice, the drink will be chilled but not watered down.

Don't misunderstand, you're certainly not limited to serving your margaritas in cocktail glasses. There are many different styles, shapes and sizes of specialty glassware from which to choose. Margaritas may also be served on-the-rocks or blended with ice. These service options require the use of different styles of glasses, but that discussion can wait for later.

• Salted Rim (optional)

Salt and tequila are traditional comrades in arms, likely because they're complementary tastes. Salting the rim of a margarita glass is more than mere embellishment, it enhances the overall drinking experience. Whatever the reason, however, many people do not want salted rims on their margaritas, making it an excellent idea to ask someone's preference before making the drink. This will spare you the shame and guilt of watching your guests wiping the salt off the glass with their fingers.

• 1 1/4 oz. Silver Tequila

It goes without saying that tequila is the featured performer in the margarita. As we'll discuss later in this chapter, there are any number of tequilas that can be used in a margarita. For this recipe, we recommend using a silver tequila, not because of its lower cost, but for its robust and vibrant character. Silver tequilas are exuberant and add a vitality to the margarita that the more reserved aged tequilas don't quite manage.

While there are those who use a shot of tequila in a margarita, we recommend a slightly healthier portion. An ounce and a quarter measure seems to best assure that guests will taste the tequila through the other ingredients without over-portioning the alcohol.

• 1/2 oz. Triple Sec

There are several options when choosing which orange-flavored liqueur to use in your "house" margarita. We'll lay out all your options later in this chapter. Generally speaking, however, if a guest orders a margarita and doesn't request a specific brand of premium tequila be used, we recommend modifying the cocktail with triple sec.

When you do use a premium tequila in a margarita, the liqueur of choice is undoubtedly Cointreau®. Its unsurpassed quality and brilliant orange flavor make it the consensus favorite. There isn't a tequila alive that wouldn't want to be married to Cointreau®.

We also suggest using a non-alcoholic triple sec, such as Rose's Triple Sec, when preparing your "house" margarita. Alcohol-free liqueurs have a better taste profile than their alcoholic counterparts, and trust us, the absence of alcohol in the triple sec won't be missed.

• 1/2 oz. Rose's Lime Juice

We recommend two ingredients most people don't think to use in their margaritas. The first is Rose's Lime Juice. A healthy splash of Rose's adds a marvelously refreshing lime flavor to the cocktail that complements the robust taste of the tequila.

Why not just use fresh lime juice? There are inconsistencies with fresh limes depending on the season and the source of the fruit. Sometimes the limes from which you have to choose are sweet and juicy, other times they're small, hard and relatively bitter, making them wholly inappropriate for use in a margarita. Rose's Lime Juice, on the other hand, is a constant, semi-sweet without the slightest trace of bitterness.

If you have some fabulously luscious limes, go ahead and squeeze the juice from a quarter of a lime into the drink. We suggest you still add a splash of Rose's for balance.

• 1/4 oz. orange juice (optional)

Adding a quarter-ounce of orange juice to a margarita—which amounts to a splash—accomplishes several things. First, the orange juice enhances the flavor of your base lemon/lime margarita mix, improving both the consistency and color of the drink. Secondly, it augments the taste of the triple sec. Go ahead, splash in some OJ.

• 1 1/2 oz. sweet 'n' sour mix

Sweet 'n' sour is used in nearly every recipe in this book. It provides the foundation for the margarita. Later in this chapter we'll cover how to create a world-class sweet 'n' sour mix of your own. Since no two scratch margarita mixes taste exactly alike, yours will become as individualized as your signature.

In the preceding margarita recipe, a jigger (1 1/2 ounces) of sweet 'n' sour mix provides just enough of a foundation to smoothly support the other ingredients without overwhelming them.

• Shake and strain

As mentioned, the margarita is a cocktail. Its ingredients need to be shaken in an iced shaker set and strained into a chilled cocktail glass. This mixing technique is used when serving the drink either straight-up or on-the-rocks.

• Fresh lime wedge garnish

Could there be a more appropriate garnish for a margarita than an ample wedge of fresh lime? Well...no. Lime wheels may look great hinged on the rim of a margarita, but they have no functional practicality. How are you supposed to squeeze the juice from a thin, circular piece of lime without it turning into a pulpy mess? Thus the reason for a wedge-shaped slice of lime. The wedge shape allows the lime juice to be easily and cleanly expressed into a drink.

If you're looking to get your margarita noticed, why not hook both a wedge and a wheel of lime on the rim of the glass? It's the best of both worlds.

There are an untold number of mixologists in this country who, whether driven personally or professionally, are on a solemn mission. They're on this mission as we speak. These magnificent warriors are steadfast on creating a signature cocktail capable of sparking the imagination and enticing all the senses. Having spent the better part of our lives behind bars, we share their passion.

The margarita makes an ideal candidate for this quest. It's versatile and can adopt an impressive array of flavors. As you're about to find out, the margarita knows no creative boundaries.

Gourmet margaritas best illustrate why leaving well enough alone is not always sound advice. This book contains well over a hundred variations of the margarita. Each is distinctively wonderful and well worth sampling. Added to our gallery of rogues are recipes submitted by some of the country's most accomplished mixologists. Unraveling the secrets of how these signature margaritas are created is the next step.

At the risk of stripping the creative process of its mystery and inspirational genius, there is a formula to engineering a high performance margarita. It involves tweaking one or more of the variables. There are ten in all. Learning how these elements affect the dynamics of the finished margarita is at the heart of the creative process.

• Tequila/Base Alcohol

Today, we have the availability of a wide variety of types, grades, and styles of tequila, far more than existed even a few years ago. There are mixtos and 100% blue agave tequilas. Within those categories there are different styles of tequila, such as blanco, reposado, and añejo. Adding to the mix, each distillery has its own house style. All of this diversity in tequilas works to the mixologist's advantage.

Every type and style of tequila creates a somewhat different tasting margarita. In the preceding margarita recipe, for instance, we chose silver tequila because of its vibrant character. Another recipe may be better suited featuring the mellow, wooded personality of an añejo tequila.

Don't hesitate to use premium tequilas in your margaritas. Committing expensive tequila to a margarita is not sacrilege, it's creative genius. We recommend when looking to use a top-shelf tequila in a gourmet margarita, you choose a recipe that adequately showcases the tequila. The recipe should have relatively few other ingredients which may tend to obscure the enhanced quality of the tequila. The cocktail should also be served straight-up to assure that there is as little dilution as possible.

We have included numerous examples of specialty margaritas that feature super-premium tequilas, recipes such as the Margarita Martini (Sauza Triada), Margarita Framboise (Porfidio Single Barrel Añejo), DC3 Margarita (Sauza Conmemorativo, Hornitos, and Tres Generaciones), and the Maximilian Margarita (Chinaco Añejo).

Then there's the technique of splitting the tequila portion in a margarita. The objective is to pair two or more complementary styles of tequila. For example, one of the specialties of the house at El Charro Café in Tucson is the Elegante Margarita. It's made with equal parts of Sauza's Conmemorativo and Hornitos. The Hornitos Reposado adds complexity and a fresh agave flavor, while the Conmemorativo Añejo contributes a spicy, well-rounded vitality to the margarita. The result is magnificent.

Other examples include the Señorita Margarita, made with a blend of Herradura Gold and Reposado tequilas, and the Margarita Mas Fino, which features both El Tesoro Silver and Añejo tequilas.

Nowhere is it written that tequila is the only distilled spirit that can be used in a margarita. The Margarita Britannia illustrates the point well. It is a surprisingly delicious margarita made with equal parts of gin and tequila. Other examples include the Normandy Margarita, which derives much of its flavor from Calvados apple brandy, and the Caribbean 'Rita, a margarita made from a blend of silver tequila and Myers's Jamaican rum.

Never one to be bound by convention, Mac Gregory, beverage director at the Hyatt Regency Scottsdale, Arizona, promotes two signature margaritas that combine tequila with unusual bed partners. The Margarita Framboise marries Porfidio Single Barrel Tequila with Bonny Doon Framboise, a sensationally flavorful, fortified raspberry wine. Another of his creations, the 'Rita La Reyna Del Playa, pairs Cuervo Reserva de la Familia Añejo with Lillet Blonde, a superb French aperitif wine.

Other creative variations of the margarita include such interesting alcoholic flavor enhancers as champagne (Mimosarita), red wine (Sangria 'Rita), and white wine (Cantina Wine Margarita).

And finally, there's the Virgin Margarita, which is prepared using no alcohol at all. Socializing without alcohol is a growing trend, so why should those good people be left out of the margarita festivities? We've provided two alcohol-free margarita recipes for such occasions. Don't scoff until you've tried them. They're not just for breakfast any more.

• Infused-Tequila Margaritas

You can turn any tequila into something extraordinary by infusing it with everything from kiwis to sun-dried tomatoes. Steeping is straight-forward and uncomplicated. The process involves marinating tequila with fresh fruit, among other things, in large, air-tight containers. Several days to a week later, the fruit will infuse the spirit with flavor, color, aroma and loads of appealing character.

One of the keys to marketing fruit-infused specialties is to put the jars somewhere conspicuous — on the back bar, for example, with big neon arrows dangling overhead. Drawing attention to the containers is part of the mystique. People will naturally be curious and ask questions about it. Anticipation will build such that, by the time it's ready to debut, there will be more than enough demand.

Any clean, presentable glass jar, ranging in capacity between 2 quarts and 2 gallons, able to maintain an air-tight seal will work. Many establishments use glass jars fitted with a brass spigot near the bottom from which the staff can draw off the precious contents.

We've provided recipes for a lime tequila infusion and a pepper tequila infusion, but the possible fruit combinations are limited only by availability. Tequila also tastes great infused with pineapples or mangos. Other interesting and exotic options include mandarin oranges, kiwis, star fruit, honeydew, papayas, watermelon, black currants, dried apricots, raspberries, and cranberries. Using a tequila that is a minimum of 80-proof will kill any bacteria present in the fruit. It is important, however, to keep the fruit completely submerged in tequila at all times. Once the fruit becomes discolored, it's best to remove it and start afresh.

Steeping tart citrus often requires the use of a sweetener. Sugar, simple syrup, or sweetened fruit juice are most frequently used to sweeten infusions, the amount is dictated by taste and personal preference. Expect the fruit to also add a natural sweetness to the spirit. In addition, raisins and maraschino cherries act as natural sweeteners.

The Pepper-Tequila Infusion (a.k.a. the Sonoran Spittoon Infusion) features tequila steeped with jalapeño peppers, a serrano chili and an assortment of green, red, and yellow bell peppers for color. After two to three days you'll have pepper-infused tequila, which in turn provides the heating element for several intriguing margaritas, including the Cajun Margarita and Margarita Picosita.

The Lime Tequila Infusion is made by steeping tequila with limes, oranges and some simple syrup. It's the headliner in the Key Lime Margarita and the Black Gold Margarita, which combines the lime-infused tequila with Sauza Conmemorativo and Chambord.

Ready to graduate to the next level? Try making the Summer Shades Margarita Infusion. This dreamy concoction is prepared by steeping gold tequila, Midori and blue Curaçao with cantaloupe, pineapples, strawberries and peaches. Taste test the infusion after several days, at which time it should have a light, fruit bouquet, a pale turquoise hue and a delightfully fresh flavor. Mix the infusion with an equivalent amount of sweet 'n' sour and shake in an iced shaker set. This specialty margarita may be served either straight-up or on-the-rocks.

Two other margarita infusions to sample are the Ice Blue Margarita Infusion, which combines tequila, Midori and blue Curaçao with limes, lemons and oranges, and the Lemontree Margarita Infusion, a citrus-infused margarita.

Infusions are among the hottest trends in the bar business. The secret to their success is that they're a fun and profitable way to create something exciting, something the competition can't duplicate. When you create a winning infusion, there's only one place to get it.

Need more convincing that featuring an infusion makes good business sense? Infusions are highly profitable, yielding profit margins between 88-92%, just slightly lower if premium spirits are used. High demand at great margins — it's an unbeatable combination.

• Modifying Liqueurs

The modifier is an essential ingredient in any cocktail. It softens the sometimes harsh, biting edge of the liquor while underscoring the spirit's natural flavor. The modifier should never dominate a recipe, rather act in a supporting role, giving a cocktail dimension and personality.

When preparing a premium margarita, Cointreau® is the consensus choice as the modifier. The French liqueur is unsurpassed in the role. Cointreau® is crystal clear, highly aromatic and imbued with a vibrant orange flavor. The advantage of using Cointreau® in a premium margarita is that the liqueur will augment the cocktail's bouquet and taste profile, but won't alter its natural color. When the pressure is on, reach for the Cointreau®.

Another modifier option is Grand Marnier. While Cointreau®

and Grand Marnier are both premium orange liqueurs, the latter is formulated with a brandy-base. Modifying a premium margarita with Grand Marnier will alter the cocktail's color and introduce the flavor of brandy. In some recipes these alterations may be welcome, in others they will only serve to mask the flavor of the tequila.

A third creative option is to split the modifier by using equal parts of Cointreau® and Grand Marnier. Several sterling examples of recipes modified by both liqueurs include the Margarita Primero Clase, Triple Gold Margarita and the thoroughly irresistible Margarita La Perseverancia.

What about triple sec? Over half of the specialty margarita recipes contained in this book call for triple sec. It is a clear, inexpensive, orange-flavored liqueur typically paired with lesser tequilas, or used in recipes in which Cointreau® or Grand Marnier would simply be lost.

As mentioned earlier, we recommend using an alcohol-free triple sec in your front-line margaritas. Their fresh, pronounced orange flavors make them ideal modifiers. Anyway, why pay for the bulk alcohol used to make most triple secs when it contributes nothing beneficial to the finished cocktail?

Fortunately for us, liqueurs run the gamut of flavor, color and cost, making them excellent modifiers. Pick a flavor and there's likely a liqueur that matches it. There are over 30 specialty margarita recipes in this book that rely on a non-orange flavored liqueur as a modifier, either acting alone or in conjunction with another liqueur.

For margarita aficionados, several brands of liqueurs have risen far beyond the call to duty. Proven margarita performers include the French black raspberry liqueur, Chambord; the Japanese honeydew liqueur, Midori; the Italian almond liqueur, Di Saronno Amaretto; and Damiana, a Mexican liqueur made from the damiana plant. Another often relied upon cordial is blue Curaçao, an orange-flavored liqueur slightly sweeter than triple sec and beloved for its luminous blue color.

Several recipes combine more than one liqueur to achieve the desired taste profile. For example, the Margarita Azul is prepared using both Di Saronno Amaretto and blue Curaçao, while the Rio Grande Margarita is made with Tia Maria and Frangelico. Rarely will adding a splash of a liqueur do anything but jazz up a margarita.

• Flavoring Agents

Remember the unlimited realm of creative possibilities we keep talking about… well, the number of ways to tweak the flavor of your gourmet margaritas is about to expand even further.

Armed with an electric blender, you can puree any fresh fruit to enhance the flavor of your specialty margaritas. The partial shopping list includes jellied cranberry sauce for the Cranberry Margarita, prickly pear marmalade for the Cactus Rose Margarita, canned Bartlett pears to make the Pearita, apple sauce for the Apple Margarita, and blueberries for the Blue Berrita Margarita. You'll also need to pick up some prickly pear juice for the Coyote Margarita, mangoes for the Mangorita, pineapples, strawberries, raspberries, bananas, and a pomegranate or two.

Another loose category of flavoring agents includes such interesting ingredients as lemon sorbet (Blue Moon Margarita), orange sorbet (Sunny Margarita), vanilla ice cream (Ice Cream Margarita), jalapeño pepper sauce (Jalapeñorita), prickly pear syrup (Prickly Pineapple Margarita), Bloody Mary mix (Bloody Margarita), and jalapeño pepper juice for the Cajun Margarita.

• Base Margarita Mix (Sweet 'n' Sour Mix)

Like a canvas to a painter, margarita mix is the foundation on which you will create your work of art. If your mix is less than wonderful, what chance do your margaritas have? Don't short circuit your efforts. Starting with a world-class margarita mix will greatly increase your odds for success.

So how do you gauge if your margarita mix (a.k.a. sweet 'n' sour mix) falls into the world-class category? Start by tasting some over ice. It should be delicious and completely devoid of any bitter or artificial aftertaste. Your sweet 'n' sour should have a light, fresh quality and be well-balanced, meaning not too sweet or tart.

As for the taste profile, there are essentially three directions you can take your sweet 'n' sour mix. The traditional slant is to use fresh lime juice. On the other hand, most bars and restaurants use a lemon-based sweet 'n' sour in their margaritas, primarily because it's also the base ingredient in other standard drinks, such as the daiquiri, Collins and sour. The third and final taste profile is attained by using both lime and lemon juice.

There are a number of commercially bottled margarita mixes, many of which are quite good. Keep in mind that you can use a commercial sweet 'n' sour and modify it to better suit your tastes. Bottled mixes do have the advantage of being stabilized for a longer shelf life. So keep your options open and don't disregard using a bottled mix.

There are also excellent reasons for devising a margarita mix from scratch, not the least of which is that no two scratch mixes taste exactly alike. Your killer scratch recipe will give your margaritas a leg up on the competition, even if your only competition is your last batch of margaritas.

Making sweet 'n' sour mix from scratch is easier than it might sound. The basic ingredients are lime or lemon juice (or both), sugar and a little water. You may have noticed that these are also the ingredients for making limeade and lemonade. For this purpose, we're looking for something not quite as sweet as limeade and lemonade.

While there is a certain cache associated with using fresh squeezed juice in your scratch mix, there are also frozen products already sweetened and far more convenient. If you use a frozen concentrate, we suggest for consistency purposes using less water than called for in the product directions. Either way you go, fresh or frozen, you will need to decide if your specialty margarita should contain pulp. [Dare we admit this is the only point that Ray and Robert couldn't agree on? According to Ray and the rest of the editorial staff, a gourmet margarita prepared with pulpy, freshly squeezed juice is a genuine mark of excellence. The older and presumably wiser Robert (rightly) considers pulp in a cocktail annoying flotsam, just another thing to get caught in the teeth and cling to the side of a glass.]

Unless you live in a community fortunate enough to have pristine tap water, we recommend using bottled or filtered water in your sweet 'n' sour mix. The water is used to thin the juice slightly and help balance out the natural tartness. Even though only a little water will be used, don't compromise the mix with hard tap water.

It's also a good idea to use simple syrup instead of granulated sugar to sweeten your sweet 'n' sour. Simple syrup is essentially dissolved sugar. Unlike granulated sugar, it will immediately go into solution instead of settling on the bottom of the container. As the name would imply, simple syrup is easy to make. Bring two cups of water to a boil in a sauce pan and stir in two cups of granulated sugar. Allow the syrup to cool before using.

Once you have all the base ingredients, begin by mixing six parts of lime or lemon juice to one part water and one part simple syrup. Taste the mix and adjust accordingly. It is unlikely you will need to add more water during the process. Better the mix have the consistency of fresh juice than too thin from being over-diluted.

As mentioned, the finished margarita mix should taste delicious in its own right. If you have an urge to improve on perfection, consider splashing in orange juice and Rose's Lime Juice for added dimension and character. Many people also enjoy the zesty effervescence a splash of either Seven-Up or Sprite adds to a margarita.

· Methods of Preparation and Presentation

One of the few similarities between the various stories of how the margarita originated is that it was born a cocktail, meaning that it was shaken and served straight-up in a chilled cocktail glass.

Over the years, drinking preferences have changed. Today it is more likely a margarita will be requested either on-the-rocks or blended with ice. Each of these methods of preparation will affect the taste, consistency and alcohol potency of the drink. A margarita straight-up is the most concentrated version of the drink, while blending it with ice is the most diluted.

The electric blender single-handedly expanded the world of margaritas. Blended margaritas (a.k.a. frozen margaritas) are as popular as ever. They're bigger than most drinks and presented with a high perceived value. The blender also affords you a fuller range of ingredient options.

For those aching to try out their blender, consider the Midnight Madness Margarita, a novel swirled-drink made in two parts, one requiring blue Curaçao and the other Chambord. The resulting drink is both delicious and visually striking. Another gourmet margarita worth being seen with is the Raspberry Torte Margarita, a blended concoction separated in the middle by a layer of luscious raspberry puree.

The Two-Toned Margarita is a delicious and remarkably clever concoction. Begin by making a Hornitos margarita and pouring half of the drink in a half-filled glass of ice. Pour the remainder of the cocktail into the blender with an added shot of Midori. Blend the drink, then layer the Midori-laced margarita on top of the lighter colored, iced Hornitos margarita. The drink has two distinctly different colored and flavored personalities. The effect is simply fantastic.

The Meltdown Margarita is made with Sauza Silver Tequila, Grand Marnier, Chambord, sweet 'n' sour, and raspberries. However, instead of blending the Chambord into the margarita, it's served separately in a shot glass for the guest to pour on top of the drink. The Chambord will slowly wind its way down through the margarita adding the marvelous flavor of raspberries and creating a striking presentation.

· Glassware

A margarita's first impression is made by the glass it is presented in, and believe it or not, the better the drink looks, the better it seems to taste. Prove it to yourself. Pour your favorite margarita into a paper cup and a hand-blown, stemmed specialty glass and see which your guests prefer. Our money is on the one with the enhanced presentation.

For margaritas served straight-up, the cocktail glass you choose should be a minimum of five-ounces in capacity. There are a wide variety of shapes and sizes from which to choose, so pick a style that best epitomizes your cocktail's personality. Serving the same cocktail on-the-rocks requires a glass with a minimum capacity of ten-ounces. Here again, there are many styles of tumblers and specialty glasses designed to accommodate iced cocktails. Choose the one that best showcases your efforts.

The largest selection of specialty glasses is reserved for your blended drinks. The possibilities range from fiesta grandes, coupettes and hurricane glasses to mason jars, wine glasses and beer mugs. If the container is transparent with a minimum capacity of fourteen-ounces, it's a candidate. After all, who says you can't serve frozen margaritas in yard glasses?

· Salting the Rim

You spend hours devising a fabulous signature margarita only to be faced with the prospect of sending it out in public dressed with an ordinary rim of coarse salt. It's embarrassing and far too pedestrian for your work of art. Fear not, the fashion police have finally solved the dilemma of the under-dressed margarita. Embellish your specialties in the style they deserve with designer salts.

High fashion has indeed hit the world of margarita salt. Now there are margarita salts marketed in different colors. *Franco's* of Pompano Beach, Florida, makers of a line of cocktail mixes, has introduced three brightly colored margarita salts, in the festive hues of blue, green and yellow. The coloring used to make *Franco's Colored Margarita Salt* are permanently adhered to the salt so they won't run or bleed, and the taste of the salt is completely unaffected by the coloring.

The *Blendex Company* of Louisville, Kentucky, also recently introduced a line of designer margarita salts in five different shades—Sunset Red, Tropical Green, Mediterranean Blue, Sunburst Yellow and Fresh Orange. You can mix the various salts together to create scores of colorful possibilities.

The *Twang* company of San Antonio, Texas,

wondered why margarita salt has to taste like, well, salt? Receiving no answer, they proceeded to create *Twangarita Margarita Salt*. These delectable salts come in three flavors—lemon/lime, pickle, and the tart and spicy chili con limon. They can be used by themselves, blended together, or mixed with your regular margarita salt. For that matter, mix some flavored salt with the colored salt.

Affixing salt to a glass is best accomplished by rimming the edge with lime juice, and then dipping the glass into a saucer of salt. The benefit to using a lime wedge to wet the rim is that the salt will only adhere to the outside of the glass, and not the interior where the salt would quickly dissolve into the margarita.

When preparing a margarita glass, consider salting only half the rim. This will allow all guests to receive a well-dressed margarita while affording them the opportunity of moderating how much salt they consume. If given the time, we recommend salting your margarita glasses in advance, allowing the lime juice and salt combination to harden somewhat. This will alleviate the messy problem of salt falling off the rim of the glass.

There are also margarita recipes that call for a sugared rim. This is typically the case with fruit margaritas, or recipes on the sweeter end of the spectrum. In the past we were limited to using conventional sugar on the rim. Those days are thankfully behind us. The Blendex company has introduced a novel line of colored sugars in red and blue. The sugar affixes easily to the rim of a glass, adding a sweet splash of color to specialty margaritas.

Another option is using powdered pink lemonade mix on the rims of margarita glasses. It has a sweet lemon flavor and an attractive color. For an entirely different presentation, rim the edge of a glass first with grenadine before dipping it into pink lemonade mix.

· Garnishing

The final touch to any noteworthy margarita is the garnish. More than a mere embellishment, the garnish should be considered an ingredient in the drink. The classic garnish for the margarita, the lime wedge, adds a delightful citrus tang that helps in balancing the drink's taste profile.

There are two mistakes many people make when garnishing their margaritas. The first is providing guests with puny limes wedges. Why sabotage your efforts by garnishing a margarita with an inadequate sliver of lime? What people want are hefty lime wedges that they can get their hands on so they can squeeze some fresh lime juice into their drink.

While there are several different ways to cut a lime wedge, here's the technique we recommend. Cut the lime in half lengthwise between its two ends. Laying the halves cut side-down on a cutting board, make two or three cuts lengthwise, from end to end, thereby producing three to four lime wedges. The number of wedges you get out of a lime is dependent on its relative size. Make a small incision in the fruit of each wedge so it can be hinged to the rim of a glass.

The second most common mistake people make when garnishing a margarita is dropping the lime wedge directly into the drink. Do they really expect their guests to fish the lime out of the drink with their fingers? Or, a bartender will first squeeze the lime wedge before dropping it into the drink. Now there's a crushed piece of fruit staring up at the guest. The appropriate move is to hook the lime wedge on the rim of the glass and allow the guest to squeeze the juice into the drink, should they choose to do so.

This is all about creative options. The realm of possible garnishes for your margarita includes a lime wheel (a circular slice of lime cut along the diameter of the fruit), lemon wedge, lemon wheel, pineapple wedge and maraschino cherry (**Caribbean 'Rita**), orange wheel (**Georgia Peach Margarita**), apple wedge (**Apple Margarita**), red raspberries (**Margarita Framboise**), small jalapeños (**Margarita Picante**), strawberry (**Cranberry Margarita**), honeydew slice (**Honeydew This Margarita**), watermelon slice (**Watermelon Margarita**), and an orange twist (**French/Russian Margarita**).

At last, the margarita recipes we've been alluding to since the beginning of the book. See, they actually exist, but wait, before you go off head first and start enjoying yourself, we feel compelled to belabor the obvious. We've arranged the following 125 recipes into categories for ease of use, and because frankly we didn't know what else to do with them.

TRADITIONAL MARGARITAS

Don't misunderstand, traditional in this context means anything but stodgy and conventional. These are creative and delicious cocktails, many of which rank among the finest in the collection.

We consider these traditional margarita recipes because they most closely conform to the model of tequila, modifier and mix. Look closely though and you'll notice many novel twists and tweaks. We think you'll gain a new found appreciation for tradition.

BLUE MARGARITA

Cocktail or house specialty glass, chilled
(Salted rim and ice optional)
1 1/4 oz. Sauza Silver Tequila
3/4 oz. Blue Curaçao
1/2 oz. Rose's Lime Juice
1 1/2 oz. sweet 'n' sour mix
Shake and strain
Fresh lime wedge garnish

CADILLAC MARGARITA

Cocktail or house specialty glass, chilled
(Salted rim and ice optional)
1 1/4 oz. Cuervo 1800 Tequila
3/4 oz. Grand Marnier
1/2 oz. Rose's Lime Juice
1 1/2 oz. sweet 'n' sour mix
Shake and strain
Fresh lime wedge garnish

El Charro Café in Tucson, Arizona is a mecca for margarita aficionados. It was also a bastion of tequila long before it was chic. The **Horny Margarita** is a specialty of the house, a classically structured cocktail featuring El Charro's best selling duo, Sauza Hornitos Reposado and Cointreau®.

GUAYMAS MARGARITA

Cocktail or house specialty glass, ice optional
(Salted rim and ice optional)
1 1/4 oz. Sauza Tres Generaciones Añejo Tequila
3/4 oz. Cointreau®
1/2 oz. Rose's Lime Juice
1 1/2 oz. sweet 'n' sour mix
Shake and strain
Fresh lime wedge garnish

HORNY MARGARITA (1)

Cocktail or house specialty glass, ice optional
(Salted rim and ice optional)
1 1/2 oz. Sauza Hornitos Reposado Tequila
1/2 oz. Cointreau®
1/4 oz. Rose's Lime Juice
2 oz. fresh lime juice
2 oz. sweet 'n' sour mix
Shake and strain
Fresh lime wedge garnish

HORNY MARGARITA (2)

Cocktail or house specialty glass, ice optional
(Salted rim and ice optional)
1 1/4 oz. Sauza Hornitos Reposado Tequila
3/4 oz. Rose's Triple Sec
1/2 oz. Rose's Lime Juice
1/2 oz. cranberry juice
1 3/4 oz. sweet 'n' sour mix
Shake and strain
Fresh lime wedge garnish

MAD RUSSIAN MARGARITA

Cocktail or house specialty glass, chilled
(Salted rim and ice optional)
  1 1/4 oz. Sauza Gold Tequila
  3/4 oz. Blue Curaçao
  1/2 oz. Grand Marnier
  1/2 oz. cranberry juice
  2 oz. sweet 'n' sour mix
  Shake and strain
  Fresh lime wedge garnish

MARGARITA CLASSICO

Cocktail or house specialty glass, chilled
(Salted rim and ice optional)
  1 1/4 oz. Silver Tequila
  1/2 oz. Rose's Triple Sec
  (1/4 oz. Rose's Lime Juice optional)
  (1/4 oz. orange juice optional)
  1 1/2 oz. sweet 'n' sour mix
  Shake and strain
  Fresh lime wedge garnish

MARGARITA DE MEXICO

Cocktail glass, chilled
(Salted rim and ice optional)
1 oz. Silver Tequila
1 oz. Controy Licor de Naranjas or Triple Sec
1 oz. fresh lime juice
Shake and strain
Fresh lime wedge garnish

Remember the margarita recipe we dissected in chapter four, here it is again, this time more appropriately dubbed the **Margarita Classico.** If you're looking for a reaction from the crowd, uncork a **Mad Russian Margarita** and watch eyebrows shoot up. Great taste in a good looking package is usually unbeatable.

MARGARITA LA PERSEVERANCIA

Cocktail glass, chilled
(Salted rim and ice optional)
  1 1/4 oz. Sauza Triada Añejo Tequila
  1/2 oz. Cointreau®
  1/2 oz. Grand Marnier
  1 1/2 oz. sweet 'n' sour mix
  Shake and strain
  Fresh lime wedge garnish

MARGARITA MARTINI

Cocktail glass, chilled
(Salted rim optional)
1 1/4 oz. Sauza Triada Añejo Tequila
1/4 oz. Cointreau®
1/4 oz. Rose's Lime Juice
1/4 oz. sweet 'n' sour mix
Shake and strain
Fresh lime wedge garnish

Master mixologist Jim Albright is the creative genius behind the savory **Margarita Martini**, the popular signature drink of Tucson's Presidio Grill.

MAXIMILIAN MARGARITA

Cocktail glass, chilled
(Salted rim optional)
1 1/4 oz. Chinaco Añejo Tequila
3/4 oz. Cointreau®
1/2 oz. Rose's Lime Juice
1/4 oz. orange juice
1 1/2 oz. sweet 'n' sour mix
Shake and strain
Fresh lime wedge garnish

MIDNIGHT MARGARITA

Cocktail or house specialty glass, chilled
(Salted rim and ice optional)
1 1/4 oz. Sauza Gold Tequila
3/4 oz. Blue Curaçao
1/4 oz. Rose's Lime Juice
1 1/2 oz. sweet 'n' sour mix
Shake and strain
Fresh lime wedge garnish

THE ORIGINAL MARGARITA™
a.k.a. MARGARITA SAMES' MARGARITA

Cocktail glass, chilled
Salted rim
1 1/2 oz. Silver Tequila
3/4 oz. Cointreau®
Juice of 1/2 a fresh lime
Shake and strain
Fresh lime wedge garnish

Make sure you also stop and visit Ms. Sames' **Original Margarita**. It's a "can't miss" attraction.

PINK CADILLAC MARGARITA

Cocktail or house specialty glass, chilled
(Salted rim and ice optional)
1 1/4 oz. Cuervo 1800 Tequila
1/2 oz. Cointreau®
1/2 oz. Rose's Lime Juice
1/2 oz. cranberry juice
1 1/2 oz. sweet 'n' sour mix
Shake and strain
Fresh lime wedge garnish

ROSARITA MARGARITA

House specialty glass, chilled
(Salted rim and ice optional)
1 1/4 oz. Sauza Conmemorativo Añejo Tequila
3/4 oz. Grand Marnier
1/2 oz. cranberry juice
1/2 oz. Rose's Lime Juice
1 1/2 oz. sweet 'n' sour mix
Shake and strain
Fresh lime wedge garnish

The high-voltage personality of the Sauza Conmemorativo Añejo absolutely shines in a multi-dimensional cocktail like the **Rosarita Margarita**. We highly recommend saving this recipe for when you're really thirsty.

SONORAN MARGARITA

Cocktail or house specialty glass, chilled
(Salted rim and ice optional)
1 1/4 oz. Sauza Tres Generaciones Añejo Tequila
3/4 oz. Grand Marnier
1/2 oz. Rose's Lime Juice
1 1/2 oz. sweet 'n' sour mix
Shake and strain
Fresh lime wedge garnish

SPLIT TEQUILA MARGARITAS

There's a creative artistry at work when combining complementary styles of tequila in a margarita. The objective is to draw upon the best characteristics of each style, adding spice and dimension to the drink not possible when using just one tequila. We think the following recipes best illustrate the technique.

El Charro Café was founded by "Great Aunt" Monica Flinn, a pioneering woman who knew her margaritas. Her spirit is reflected in the **El Charro Margarita de Casa**. We hear she also liked to sip martinis out of a teacup.

DC 3 MARGARITA

Cocktail or house specialty glass, chilled
(Salted rim and ice optional)
3/4 oz. Sauza Conmemorativo Añejo Tequila
3/4 oz. Sauza Hornitos Reposado Tequila
1/2 oz. Cointreau®
1/2 oz. Rose's Lime Juice
1 oz. lemon/lime soda
1 1/4 oz. sweet 'n' sour mix
Shake and strain
Float 1/2 oz. Sauza Tres Generaciones Añejo
Fresh lime wedge garnish

EL CHARRO MARGARITA DE CASA

Cocktail or house specialty glass, chilled
(Salted rim and ice optional)
3/4 oz. Sauza Gold Tequila
3/4 oz. Sauza Silver Tequila
1/2 oz. Rose's Triple Sec
1/4 oz. Rose's Lime Juice
1/4 oz. orange juice
1 1/2 oz. sweet 'n' sour mix
Shake and strain
Fresh lime wedge garnish

EL CONQUISTADOR  MARGARITA

Cocktail or house specialty glass, chilled
 (Salted rim and ice optional)
  3/4 oz. Sauza Conmemorativo Añejo Tequila
  3/4 oz. Sauza Hornitos Reposado Tequila
  1/2 oz. Chambord
  1/2 oz. Rose's Triple Sec
  1/2 oz. Rose's Lime Juice
  1 1/2 oz. sweet 'n' sour mix
  1 1/2 oz. pineapple juice
  Shake and strain
  Fresh lime wedge garnish

ELEGANTE MARGARITA

Cocktail or house specialty glass, chilled
 (Salted rim and ice optional)
  3/4 oz. Sauza Conmemorativo Añejo Tequila
  3/4 oz. Sauza Hornitos Reposado Tequila
  1/2 oz. Cointreau®
  1/2 oz. Rose's Lime Juice
  1 1/2 oz. sweet 'n' sour mix
Shake and strain
Fresh lime wedge garnish

MARGARITA MAS FINO

Cocktail or house specialty glass, chilled
 (Salted rim and ice optional)
  3/4 oz. El Tesoro Añejo Tequila
  3/4 oz. El Tesoro Silver Tequila
  3/4 oz. Cointreau®
  1/2 oz. orange juice
  1/2 oz. Rose's Lime Juice
  1 1/2 oz. sweet 'n' sour mix
  Shake and strain
   Fresh lime wedge garnish

There's too many highly rated performers here for you to continue on to page 56 without having given each a fair and unhurried audition. The **Elegante Margarita** is one of the most popular specialties at ¡TOMA!® in El Charro Café, Tucson. Sip one and find out why.

SEÑORITA MARGARITA

House specialty glass
(Salted rim and ice optional)
1 1/4 oz. Herradura Gold Tequila
1/2 oz. Cointreau®
1/4 oz. Rose's Lime Juice
1/4 oz. fresh lime juice
1 1/2 oz. sweet 'n' sour mix
Shake and strain
Float 3/4 oz. Herradura Reposado Tequila
Fresh lime wedge garnish

Reposados are the best-selling style of tequila in Mexico, a country that knows its tequila. These specialties honor the regal reposado by saving him the best seat in the house.

Z-RATED MARGARITA

Cocktail or house specialty glass
(Salted rim and ice optional)
1/2 oz. Zafarrancho Silver Tequila
1/2 oz. Zafarrancho Gold Tequila
1/2 oz. Cointreau®
1/2 oz. Rose's Lime Juice
1/2 oz. orange juice
1 1/2 oz. sweet 'n' sour mix
Shake and strain
Float 1/2 oz. Zafarrancho Reposado Tequila
Fresh lime wedge garnish

PEPPERED MARGARITAS

Nothing goes better with great margaritas than Mexican food. These exceptionally creative recipes are simply an extension of that thought. Peppers, chilies and spices are welcome additions in a margarita, adding more flavor than heat.

Notice also that several of the recipes call for pepper-infused tequila. What could be more efficient? We also provide you with an outstanding recipe for infusing tequila, an infusion known inexplicably in some circles as the Sonoran Spittoon.

BLOODY MARGARITA
House specialty glass, ice
(Salt and pepper rim, ice optional)
1 1/4 oz. Silver Tequila
3/4 oz. Rose's Triple Sec
1/2 oz. Rose's Lime Juice
1/4 oz. jalapeño pepper juice
1-2 dashes Tabasco sauce
2 oz. Sauza Sangrita Mix
Shake and strain
Sprinkle ground habanero chile (use sparingly)
Fresh lime wedge garnish

CAJUN MARGARITA
Cocktail or house specialty glass
(Salt and pepper rim, ice optional)
1 1/4 oz. Pepper-infused Silver Tequila
1-2 dashes Tabasco sauce
1-2 dashes jalapeño pepper juice
2 oz. sweet 'n' sour mix
Shake and strain
Small jalapeño peppers garnish

COYOTE MARGARITA (1)

Cocktail or house specialty glass
(Salt and pepper rim, ice optional)
1 1/4 oz. Gold Tequila
1/2 oz. Rose's Triple Sec
1/2 oz. Rose's Lime Juice
1/4 oz. jalapeño pepper juice
1 oz. cranberry juice
1 1/2 oz. sweet 'n' sour mix
Shake and strain
Fresh lime wedge garnish

A splash of jalapeño pepper
juice adds just enough heat
to the finish of the
Coyote Margarita
to make things really interesting.

JALAPEÑORITA

House specialty glass, ice
(Salt and pepper rim optional)
1 1/4 oz. Gold Tequila
3/4 oz. Grand Marnier
1/2 tsp. Tabasco jalapeño sauce
2 oz. sweet 'n' sour mix
Shake and strain
Fresh lime wedge garnish

MARGARITA PICANTE

Cocktail or house specialty glass, chilled
(Salt and pepper rim, ice optional)
3/4 oz. Sauza Hornitos Reposado Tequila
3/4 oz. Absolut Peppar Vodka
1/2 oz. Rose's Triple Sec
1-2 dashes Tabasco sauce
2 pinches ground black pepper
4-6 drops jalapeño pepper juice
2 oz. sweet 'n' sour mix
Shake and strain
Small jalapeño peppers garnish

MARGARITA  PICOSITA

Cocktail or house specialty glass
(Salt and pepper rim, ice optional)
3/4 oz. Silver Tequila
3/4 oz. Pepper-infused Silver Tequila
1/2 oz. Rose's Triple Sec
1/2 oz. Rose's Lime Juice
1/2 oz. orange juice
1 3/4 oz. sweet 'n' sour mix
Shake and strain
Fresh lime wedge & small
    jalapeño pepper garnish

Here it is,
the recipe for
**pepper-infused
tequila.**
Moderate the
infusion's
thermostat by
paying close
attention to the
serrano chili. It
packs a wallop for
being such a
puny package.

PEPPER-TEQUILA INFUSION
a.k.a. SONORAN SPITTOON INFUSION

Fill jar 1/4 full with red bell peppers
Fill jar 1/4 full with green bell peppers
Fill jar 1/4 full with yellow bell peppers
4-6 jalapeño peppers
1 serrano chili
2 liters Gold tequila
Place washed bell peppers into jar. Lance jalapeño peppers & place
in jar along with the serrano chili. Add tequila. Test after 2-3 days.

SONORAN SPITTOON MARGARITA

Cocktail or house specialty glass
(Salt and pepper rim, ice optional)
1 1/4 oz. Pepper-infused Silver Tequila
1/2 oz. Rose's Triple Sec
1/2 oz. Rose's Lime Juice
1 1/2 oz. sweet 'n' sour mix
Shake and strain
Fresh lime wedge & small jalapeño pepper garnish

LIME INFUSED-TEQUILA MARGARITAS

Tequila infused with fresh limes...no stretch of the imagination there. In fact, it tastes absolutely fabulous. Once again, we've thought of everything and provided you with an award-winning lime-tequila infusion recipe. Well, it didn't actually win an award, but it could if there were awards for such things.

We would be deficient hosts if we didn't ask you to stop for a moment and take notice of the **Black Gold Margarita**. Lime-infused tequila, Conmemorativo Añejo and Chambord make for an irresistible collaboration.

BLACK GOLD MARGARITA

Cocktail or house specialty glass, chilled
(Salted rim and ice optional)
1 oz. Sauza Conmemorativo Añejo Tequila
1 oz. Lime-infused Sauza Silver Tequila
3/4 oz. Chambord
1/4 oz. Rose's Lime Juice
1 1/4 oz. sweet 'n' sour mix
Shake and strain
Fresh lime wedge garnish

KEY LIME MARGARITA

Cocktail or house specialty glass, chilled
(Salted rim and ice optional)
1 1/4 oz. Lime-infused Sauza Silver Tequila
1/2 oz. Rose's Triple Sec
1/4 oz. Rose's Lime Juice
1 1/2 oz. sweet 'n' sour mix
Shake and strain
Fresh lime wedge garnish

LIME-TEQUILA INFUSION

Fill jar 1/3 full with limes
Fill jar 1/3 full with oranges
Add 6 oz. simple syrup
2 liters Sauza Silver Tequila
Slice lime and oranges into rings, and layer in jar.
Add simple syrup and tequila. Test after 2-3 days.

MARGARITAS MADE WITH TEQUILA & OTHER SPIRITS

This is another example of thinking outside of the box. Using different types of spirits in margaritas as flavoring agents is innovative and down-right clever. It's a shame we didn't think of it.

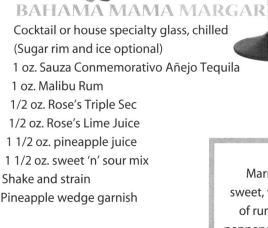

BAHAMA MAMA MARGARITA

Cocktail or house specialty glass, chilled
(Sugar rim and ice optional)
1 oz. Sauza Conmemorativo Añejo Tequila
1 oz. Malibu Rum
1/2 oz. Rose's Triple Sec
1/2 oz. Rose's Lime Juice
1 1/2 oz. pineapple juice
1 1/2 oz. sweet 'n' sour mix
Shake and strain
Pineapple wedge garnish

CARIBBEAN RITA

Cocktail or house specialty glass, chilled
(Pink lemonade mix rim and ice optional)
1 oz. Silver Tequila
1 oz. Myers's Jamaican Rum
1/2 oz. Rose's Triple Sec
1/2 oz. Rose's Lime Juice
1 1/2 oz. orange juice
1 1/2 oz. sweet 'n' sour mix
Pineapple wedge and cherry garnish

Marrying the sweet, warm flavor of rum with the peppery, herbaceous taste of tequila is what gives the Bahama Mama Margarita and the Caribbean Rita their balmy, sublime personality.

KAMI 'RITA

Cocktail or house specialty glass, chilled
(Salted rim optional)
1 oz. Sauza Hornitos Reposado Tequila
1 oz. Absolut Citron
1/2 oz. Cointreau®
1/2 oz. Rose's Lime Juice
1 1/2 oz. sweet 'n' sour mix
Shake and strain
Fresh lime wedge garnish

MARGARITA BRITANNIA

Cocktail or house specialty glass,
ice optional
3/4 oz. Silver Tequila
3/4 oz. Gin
1/2 oz. Rose's Triple Sec
1 1/2 oz. sweet 'n' sour mix
Shake and strain
Fresh lime wedge garnish

NORMANDY MARGARITA
a.k.a. APPLE MARGARITA

Cocktail or house specialty glass, chilled
(Cinnamon-sugar rim optional)
1 oz. Sauza Silver Tequila
1 oz. VS Calvados Apple Brandy
1/2 oz. Rose's Triple Sec
1/2 oz. apple juice or cider
(1/2 oz. apple sauce optional)
1 1/2 oz. sweet 'n' sour mix
Shake and strain, or blend with ice
Apple wedge garnish

Mixing together gin and tequila in the **Margarita Britannia** is an example of thinking outside the box. The result is a singularly refreshing and flavorful cocktail. Also take notice of the **Normandy Margarita** and its imaginative blend of tequila, Calvados apple brandy, and apple cider. It works!

PRESIDENTE MARGARITA

Cocktail or house specialty glass, chilled
(Salted rim and ice optional)
   1 oz. Sauza Tres Generaciones Añejo Tequila
   1 oz. Presidente Brandy
   1/2 oz. Cointreau®
   1/4 oz. fresh orange juice
   1/2 oz. Rose's Lime Juice
   2 oz. sweet 'n' sour mix
   Shake and strain
   Float 1/2 oz. Grand Marnier
   Fresh lime wedge and orange wheel garnish

The **Presidente Margarita** would make an appropriate aperitif at an official state dinner. Talk about a foreign relations coup. Presidente Brandy and Tres Generaciones Añejo obviously speak the same language. Interpreters need not apply.

We don't want to be accused of spreading unfounded rumors, but the Damiana Liqueur used to flavor the **Baja Margarita** is thought to be an aphrodisiac. Now mind you, that's what we heard.

CREATIVE MODIFIERS

Where is it written that you can only modify a margarita with an orange-flavored liqueur? And who said you could only use one modifier per recipe? In a democracy you're free to make your margaritas any way you want. Try these on for size.

BAJA MARGARITA
a.k.a. DAMIANA MARGARITA

Cocktail or house specialty glass
(Salted rim and ice optional)
   1 1/4 oz. Sauza Gold Tequila
   3/4 oz. Damiana Liqueur
   1 1/2 oz. sweet 'n' sour mix
   Shake and strain
   Fresh lime wedge garnish

BLACK FOREST MARGARITA
a.k.a. BLACK CHERRY MARGARITA
Cocktail or house specialty glass, ice optional
(Salted rim optional)
1 1/4 oz. Gold Tequila
3/4 oz. Cherry Schnapps
1/2 oz. Rose's Lime Juice
2 oz. sweet 'n' sour mix
2 oz. orange juice
Shake and strain
Fresh lime wedge garnish

CAMINO REAL MARGARITA
Cocktail or house specialty glass, chilled
(Salted rim optional)
1 1/4 oz. Silver Tequila
3/4 oz. Creme de Banana
1 oz. Rose's Lime Juice
1 oz. orange juice
1 oz. sweet 'n' sour mix
Shake and strain
Fresh lime wedge garnish

> To rim a glass with margarita salt like a pro, rub a lime wedge around the outside of the glass and gently invert it into the salt.

CATALINA MARGARITA
Cocktail or house specialty glass, chilled
(Sugar rim optional)
1 1/4 oz. Gold Tequila
1/2 oz. Blue Curaçao
1/2 oz. Peach Schnapps
1/4 oz. Rose's Lime Juice
2 oz. sweet 'n' sour mix
Shake and strain
Fresh lime wedge garnish

> The lime juice will affix the salt to the outside of the glass, preventing it from falling into your margarita.

DIABLO MARGARITA
a.k.a. RED HOT MARGARITA
Cocktail or house specialty glass,
ice optional
(Cinnamon & sugar rim optional)
1 1/4 oz. Gold Tequila
3/4 oz. Cinnamon Schnapps
1/2 oz. Rose's Lime Juice
1 1/2 oz. orange juice
1 1/2 oz. sweet 'n' sour mix
Shake and strain
Fresh lime wedge garnish

GEORGIA MARGARITA

Cocktail or house specialty glass, chilled
(Sugar rim and ice optional)
1 1/4 oz. Silver Tequila
3/4 oz. Peach Schnapps
1/2 oz. Rose's Lime Juice
1 1/2 oz. sweet 'n' sour mix
Shake and strain
Fresh lime wedge garnish

GEORGIA PEACH MARGARITA

Cocktail or house specialty glass, chilled
(Sugar rim and ice optional)
1 1/4 oz. Sauza Conmemorativo Añejo Tequila
1/2 oz. Peach Schnapps
1/2 oz. Rose's Triple Sec
1/2 oz. Rose's Lime Juice
1 1/2 oz. orange juice
1 1/2 oz. sweet 'n' sour mix
Shake and strain
Orange wheel garnish

Do not proceed to page 66 until you've at least seriously considered sampling the Italian Margarita. It is a classic margarita. The nutty almond-flavor of Di Saronno Amaretto provides an ideal counterpoint to the taste of the gold tequila.

ITALIAN MARGARITA

Cocktail or house specialty glass, chilled
(Sugar rim and ice optional)
1 1/4 oz. Gold Tequila
3/4 oz. Di Saronno Amaretto
1/2 oz. Rose's Triple Sec
1/2 oz., orange juice
2 oz. sweet 'n' sour mix
Shake and strain
Orange wheel, cherry and lime wedge garnish

The **Margarita Framboise** is a specialty of the Hyatt Regency Scottsdale at Gainey Ranch. It was masterminded by Mac Gregory, beverage director of the upscale resort. Also earning five-star recommendation are the **Teal Margarita** and **Margarita Azul**. Both are as beautiful to look at as they are delicious to drink.

LUNA AZUL MARGARITA

Cocktail or house specialty glass, chilled
(Salted rim and ice optional)
1 1/4 oz. Luna Azul Reposado Tequila
1/2 oz. Cointreau®
1/2 oz. Blue Curaçao
1/2 oz. Rose's Lime Juice
1 1/2 oz. sweet 'n' sour mix
Shake and strain
Fresh lime wedge garnish

MARGARITA AZUL

Cocktail glass, chilled
(Salted rim optional)
1 1/4 oz. Sauza Hornitos Reposado Tequila
1/2 oz. Di Saronno Amaretto
1/2 oz. Blue Curaçao
1/4 oz. fresh lime juice
1 1/2 oz. sweet 'n' sour mix
Shake and strain
Fresh lime wedge garnish

MARGARITA FRAMBOISE

Cocktail or house specialty glass, chilled
(Salt and sugar rim, ice optional)
1 1/2 oz. Porfidio Single Barrel Añejo Tequila
3/4 oz. Bonny Doon Framboise (Raspberry) Wine
1/4 oz. Cointreau®
1/4 oz. Grand Marnier
1/2 oz. fresh lime juice
1/4 oz. orange juice
2 oz. sweet 'n' sour mix
Shake and strain
Lime wheel and floated red raspberries garnish

MARGARITA PRIMERO CLASE

Cocktail or house specialty glass
(Salted rim and ice optional)
  1 1/4 oz. El Tesoro Añejo Tequila
  1/2 oz. Cointreau®
  1/2 oz. Grand Marnier
  1/2 oz. Rose's Lime Juice
  1 1/2 oz. sweet 'n' sour mix
  Shake and strain
  Fresh lime wedge garnish

MELON MARGARITA
a.k.a. GREEN IGUANA

Cocktail or house specialty glass, chilled
(Salted rim and ice optional)
  1 oz. Sauza Hornitos Reposado Tequila
  1 oz. Midori
  1 1/2 oz. sweet 'n' sour mix
 Shake and strain
 Fresh lime wedge garnish

> Do not under any circumstances pass through your formative adult years without trying a Green Iguana, or as it is more commonly known, the Melon Margarita. Midori and Sauza Hornitos are a perfectly matched couple.

PURPLE MARGARITA
a.k.a. PURPLE HAZE MARGARITA

Cocktail or house specialty glass, chilled
(Salted rim and ice optional)
  1 1/4 oz. Gold Tequila
  1/2 oz. Blue Curaçao
  1/2 oz. Chambord
  1/2 oz. Rose's Lime Juice
  1 oz. cranberry juice
  1 1/2 oz. sweet 'n' sour mix
  Shake and strain
  Fresh lime wedge garnish

OSCARITA MARGARITA

House specialty glass
(Sugar rim and ice optional)
  1 1/4 oz. Sauza Gold Tequila
  1/2 oz. Cointreau®
  1/4 oz. Grand Marnier
  1/4 oz. Di Saronno Amaretto
  1 1/2 oz. orange juice
  1 1/2 oz. sweet 'n' sour mix
  Shake and strain
  Fresh lime wedge garnish

RIO GRANDE MARGARITA

Cocktail or house specialty glass, chilled
(Salted rim and ice optional)
3/4 oz. Sauza Hornitos Reposado Tequila
3/4 oz. Tia Maria
3/4 oz. Frangelico Liqueur
1 1/2 oz. orange juice
1 1/2 oz. sweet 'n' sour mix
Shake and strain
Fresh lime wedge garnish

The **Purple Margarita** is a guaranteed crowd pleaser. Aside from being delicious, the ingredients meld together to create the most captivating, deep-purple colored cocktail. The **'Rita la Reyna del Playa** is also the brainchild of Mac Gregory, beverage guru of the Hyatt Regency Scottsdale.

'RITA LA REYNA DEL PLAYA

Cocktail or house specialty glass, chilled
(Salted rim and ice optional)
1 1/2 oz. Cuervo Reserva de la Familia Añejo
3/4 oz. Lillet Blonde
1/2 oz. Midori
1/4 oz. pineapple juice
1/4 oz. orange juice
2 oz. sweet 'n' sour mix
Shake and strain
Orange wheel and lime wedge garnish

SANTA RITA MARGARITA

Cocktail or house specialty glass, chilled
(Salted rim and ice optional)
1 1/4 oz. Gold Tequila
1/2 oz. Chambord
1/2 oz. Peach Schnapps
2 oz. sweet 'n' sour mix
Shake and strain
Fresh lime wedge garnish

SANTIAGO MARGARITA

Cocktail or house specialty glass
(Pink lemonade mix rim, ice optional)
- 1 1/4 oz. Silver Tequila
- 3/4 oz. Midori
- 1/2 oz. Rose's Triple Sec
- 1/2 oz. Rose's Lime Juice
- 1/4 oz. grenadine
- 1 1/2 oz. grapefruit juice
- 2 oz. sweet 'n' sour mix
- Shake and strain
- Orange wheel garnish

> If you're a devotee of unadorned beauty, we suggest the altogether satisfying Spanish Margarita. If you want something tall and luscious, try the Santiago Margarita— but if you walk on the wild side, hitch your star to the Triple Gold Margarita.

SPANISH MARGARITA
a.k.a. GOLD RUSH MARGARITA

Cocktail or house specialty glass
(Salted rim and ice optional)
- 1 1/2 oz. Gold Tequila
- 3/4 oz. Licor 43 (Cuarenta y Tres)
- 1/2 oz. Rose's Lime Juice
- 1 1/2 oz. sweet 'n' sour mix
- Shake and strain
- Fresh lime wedge garnish

TEAL MARGARITA

Cocktail or house specialty glass, chilled
(Salted rim and ice optional)
- 1 1/4 oz. Sauza Hornitos Reposado Tequila
- 1/2 oz. Grand Marnier
- 1/2 oz. Blue Curaçao
- 1/2 oz. cranberry juice
- 1 1/2 oz. sweet 'n' sour mix
- Shake and strain
- Fresh lime wedge garnish

TRIPLE GOLD MARGARITA

Cocktail or house specialty glass
(Salted rim and ice optional)
1 1/2 oz. Gold Tequila
1/4 oz. Cointreau®
1/4 oz. Grand Marnier
1 1/2 oz. sweet 'n' sour mix
Shake and strain
Float 1/2 oz. Goldschläger
Fresh lime wedge garnish

TUACA MARGARITA

Cocktail or house specialty glass, chilled
(Sugar rim and ice optional)
1 oz. Silver Tequila
1 oz. Tuaca
1 1/2 oz. sweet 'n' sour mix
(Splash lemon/lime soda optional)
Shake and strain
Fresh lime wedge garnish

If you're looking to get the most bang out of your limes, before juicing or cutting them into wedges, run the lime under warm water. Apparently they like the attention because they yield more juice afterwards.

CREATIVE USE OF FLAVORING AGENTS

Flavoring agents give a margarita its own singular personality. A dash of this, a scoop of that and before you know it you've really got something to brag about. It's usually a modest ingredient, a minor player in the scheme of things, but as you'll see, it's often just enough to propel the ordinary into the extraordinary.

AGAVE JUICE MARGARITA

Cocktail or house specialty glass
(Salted rim and ice optional)
1 1/4 oz. Sauza Hornitos Reposado Tequila
1/2 oz. Rose's Triple Sec
1/2 oz. Rose's Lime Juice
1-2 dashes angostura bitters
1/2 oz. grenadine
1 oz. orange juice
1 oz. sweet 'n' sour mix
Shake and strain
Fresh lime wedge garnish

BLUE MOON MARGARITA

House specialty glass, chilled
(Salted rim and ice optional)
1 1/4 oz. Sauza Conmemorativo Añejo Tequila
3/4 oz. Blue Curaçao
1/2 oz. Rose's Lime Juice
1-2 scoops lemon sorbet
1 1/2 oz. sweet 'n' sour mix
Blend with ice
Fresh lime wedge garnish

The **Blue Moon Margarita** is an absolute no-brainer. Blending lemon sorbet into a margarita is a stroke of genius. In fact, we're going to take full credit for the idea, that is until the rightful owner of this innovative notion steps forward.

CHAPALA MARGARITA

Cocktail or house specialty glass
(Salted rim and ice optional)
1 1/4 oz. Herradura Gold Tequila
1/2 oz. Cointreau®
1/2 oz. orange juice
1/2 oz. Rose's Lime Juice
1/4 oz. grenadine
1-2 dashes of orange flower water
1 1/2 oz. sweet 'n' sour mix
Shake and strain
Fresh lime wedge garnish

COYOTE MARGARITA (2)

Cocktail or house specialty glass
(Salt and pepper rim, ice optional)
1 1/2 oz. Sauza Conmemorativo Añejo Tequila
1/2 oz. Rose's Triple Sec
1/2 oz. Rose's Lime Juice
1 1/2 oz. prickly pear juice
1 1/2 oz. sweet 'n' sour mix
Shake and strain
Fresh lime wedge garnish

The Floridita 'Rita was the specialty of the house at the Blue Moon Cafe in Tucson. It unfortunately is no longer with us, but we still have Jeff Spiri's marvelous concoction. Need more creative inspiration? How about scooping together an Ice Cream Margarita, or muddling your way into an Herba Buena Margarita?

FLORIDITA 'RITA

a.k.a. FLORIDA MARGARITA

Cocktail or house specialty glass
(Pink lemonade mix rim optional)
1 1/4 oz. Sauza Hornitos Reposado Tequila
1/2 oz. Rose's Triple Sec
1/2 oz. cranberry juice
1/4 oz. Rose's Lime Juice
1 1/2 oz. grapefruit juice
1 1/2 oz. sweet 'n' sour mix
Shake and strain
Fresh lime wedge garnish

HERBA BUENA MARGARITA

a.k.a. MARGARITA MOJITO

Tall house specialty glass, ice recommended
(Salted rim optional)
5-6 sprigs fresh mint leaves
Splash simple syrup
1 1/4 oz. Sauza Conmemorativo Añejo Tequila
1/2 oz. Rose's Triple Sec
1/2 oz. Rose's Lime Juice
2 oz. lemon/lime soda
2 oz. sweet 'n' sour mix
Shake and strain
Fresh mint springs and lime wedge garnish
Muddle (crush) mint leaves with simple syrup
in the specialty glass. Add ice to the glass and
strain in the other reciped ingredients.

ICE CREAM MARGARITA

House specialty glass
1 1/4 oz. Gold Tequila
3/4 oz. Creme de Banana
1/2 oz. Rose's Triple Sec
1-2 scoops vanilla ice cream
2 oz. sweet 'n' sour mix
Blend with ice
Orange slice and cherry garnish

LA BAMBA MARGARITA

Cocktail or house specialty glass
 (Sugar rim and ice optional
   1 1/4 oz. Sauza Conmemorativo Añejo Tequila
   1/2 oz. Cointreau®
   1/4 oz. grenadine
   1 1/2 oz. pineapple juice
   1 1/2 oz. orange juice
   Shake and strain
   Fresh lemon wedge garnish

MARGARITA SPLASH

House specialty glass, ice
(Salted rim optional)
1 1/4 oz. Sauza Silver Tequila
1/2 oz. Rose's Triple Sec
1 1/2 oz. fresh lime juice
1 1/2 oz. sweet 'n' sour mix
Shake and strain
Fill with club soda
Fresh lime wedge garnish

> If you're in the market for a thirst quenching summer specialty, the consensus favorite is the **Margarita Splash**, a tall, iced marvel brimming with spirit and effervescence.

MAUI MARGARITA (1)

House specialty glass, chilled
(Salted rim and ice optional)
1 1/4 oz. Sauza Gold Tequila
1/2 oz. Rose's Triple Sec
1/2 oz. Rose's Lime Juice
1 1/2 oz. orange juice
2 oz. sweet 'n' sour mix
Blend with ice
Fresh lime wedge garnish

MAUI MARGARITA (2)

Cocktail or house specialty glass, chilled
(Salted rim and ice optional)
1 1/4 oz. Sauza Gold Tequila
3/4 oz. Grand Marnier
1/2 oz. pineapple juice
1 1/2 oz. sweet 'n' sour mix
Shake and strain
Fresh lime wedge garnish

ORANGITA MARGARITA

Cocktail or house specialty glass, chilled
(Sugar rim and ice optional)
1 1/4 oz. Sauza Gold Tequila
1/2 oz. Rose's Triple Sec
1/4 oz. Rose's Lime Juice
1/2 oz. sweet 'n' sour mix
1 1/2 oz. orange juice
Shake and strain
Fresh lime wedge garnish

PINK MARGARITA

Cocktail or house specialty glass, chilled
(Salted rim and ice optional)
1 1/4 oz. Silver Tequila
3/4 oz. Rose's Triple Sec
1/2 oz. Rose's Lime Juice
1/2 oz. grenadine
1 1/2 oz. sweet 'n' sour mix
Shake and strain
Fresh lime wedge garnish

PRICKLY PEAR MARGARITAS

(1)

House specialty glass
(Salted rim and ice optional)
1 1/4 oz. Sauza Silver Tequila
1/2 oz. Rose's Triple Sec
1/2 oz. Rose's Lime Juice
1/4 oz. grenadine
3/4 oz. prickly pear juice
1 1/2 oz. sweet 'n' sour mix
Blend with ice
Fresh lime wedge garnish

(2)

House specialty glass, chilled
(Salted rim and ice optional)
1 1/4 oz. Sauza Silver Tequila
1/2 oz. Rose's Triple Sec
3/4 oz. Rose's Lime Juice
1 1/2 oz. prickly pear juice
2 oz. sweet 'n' sour mix
Blend with ice
Fresh lime wheel garnish

How can something so sweet and delicious like prickly pear juice come from such a formidable looking cactus? We have no idea, but these two prickly pear margaritas are well worth the pain of harvest time.

PRICKLY PINEAPPLE MARGARITA

Cocktail glass, chilled
(Salted rim and ice optional)
1 1/4 oz. Sauza Conmemorativo Añejo Tequila
1/2 oz. Grand Marnier
1/2 oz. prickly pear syrup
3/4 oz. pineapple juice
1 1/2 oz. sweet 'n' sour mix
Shake and strain
Fresh lime wedge garnish

SUNNY MARGARITA

House specialty glass, chilled
(Salted rim and ice optional)
1 1/4 oz. Sauza Gold Tequila
3/4 oz. Rose's Triple Sec
1/2 oz. Rose's Lime Juice
2 scoops orange sorbet
2 oz. sweet 'n' sour mix
Blend with ice
Fresh lime wedge garnish

Whether you use Earl Grey or Sleepytime®, the Tea-arita Margarita is a

TEA-ARITA MARGARITA

Tall house specialty glass, ice recommended
(Salted rim optional)
1 1/4 oz. Sauza Silver Tequila
1/2 oz. Rose's Triple Sec
1/2 oz. Rose's Lime Juice
2 oz. iced tea
2 oz. sweet 'n' sour mix
Shake and strain
Fresh lemon and lime wedge garnish

taste-tested thirst buster, a veteran of combat on verandas and hammocks across the country.

TRES COMPADRES MARGARITA

Cocktail or house specialty glass, chilled
(Salted rim and ice optional)
1 1/4 oz. Sauza Conmemorativo Añejo Tequila
1/2 oz. Cointreau®
1/2 oz. Chambord
1/2 oz. Rose's Lime Juice
3/4 oz. fresh lime juice
3/4 oz. orange juice
3/4 oz. grapefruit juice
Shake and strain
Fresh lime wedge garnish

BLENDED FRUIT MARGARITAS

There's at least one margarita pundit who contends that blended margaritas are nothing but slushy counterfeits, to which we reply, balderdash! Blending fresh fruit into a margarita is a stroke of creative genius, and there's no other way to suck fruit throw a straw than to blend it first. Sample a few of these blended marvels and see what you think.

BLUE BERRITA MARGARITA

House specialty glass
(Blue salt rim optional)
1 1/4 oz. Silver Tequila
1/2 oz. Blue Curaçao
1/2 oz. Chambord
1/2 oz. Rose's Triple Sec
1/2 oz. Rose's Lime Juice
1/4 cup frozen blueberries
2 oz. sweet 'n' sour mix
Blend with ice
Fresh lime wedge garnish

The Blue Berrita Margarita is the brainchild of the imaginative minds at the Food Group in New York, the nation's leading food service marketing agency. These creative gurus also devised such delicious libations as the Bahama Mama Margarita and the Caribbean 'Rita.

CACTUS ROSE MARGARITA

House specialty glass, chilled
(Sugar rim optional)
1 1/4 oz. Sauza Gold Tequila
1/2 oz. Grand Marnier
1/2 oz. Chambord
1/2 oz. Rose's Lime Juice
1/4 cup frozen raspberries
1 oz. cranberry juice
2 oz. sweet 'n' sour mix
Blend with ice
Fresh lime wedge garnish

CRANBERRY MARGARITA (1)

House specialty glass, chilled
(Salted rim optional)
1 1/2 oz. Sauza Silver Tequila
1/2 oz. Rose's Triple Sec
3/4 oz. Rose's Lime Juice
3/4 oz. sweet 'n' sour mix
2 oz. cranberry juice
2 oz. strawberry puree
Blend with ice
Fresh lime wedge garnish

CRANBERRY MARGARITA (2)

House specialty glass, chilled
(Sugar rim optional)
  1 1/2 oz. Sauza Silver Tequila
  1/2 oz. Rose's Triple Sec
  1/4 cup jellied cranberry sauce
  1 1/2 oz. sweet 'n' sour mix
  Blend with ice
  Fresh strawberry garnish

HAWAIIAN MARGARITA
a.k.a. GIGGLING MARGARITA

House specialty glass, chilled
(Sugar rim optional)
  1 1/4 oz. Sauza Silver Tequila
  1/2 oz. Di Saronno Amaretto
  1/2 oz. Blue Curaçao
  3-4 slices of cored pineapple
  2 oz. sweet 'n' sour mix
  Blend with ice
  Pineapple and fresh lime wedge garnish

Ready to rev up your blender? One piece of advice. Most people do not blend their margaritas long enough for the ice to be completely homogenized with the reciped ingredients. Use a scoop of ice, and then let the blender do its thing. No hurry, no worry.

HONEYDEW THIS MARGARITA

House specialty glass, chilled
(Sugar rim optional)
1 1/4 oz. Sauza Gold Tequila
1/2 oz. Rose's Lime Juice
1/2 cup diced honeydew melon
2 oz. sweet 'n' sour mix
Blend with ice
Honeydew slice garnish

MANGO MARGARITA
a.k.a. MANGORITA

House specialty glass, chilled
(Salted rim optional)
1 1/4 oz. Sauza Gold Tequila
1/2 cup fresh mango chunks
1/2 oz. Rose's Lime Juice
2 oz. sweet 'n' sour mix
Blend with ice
Fresh lime wedge garnish

MARGARITA DE FRUTA

House specialty glass, chilled
(Sugar rim optional)
1 1/4 oz. Sauza Silver Tequila
1/2 oz. Rose's Triple Sec
1/2 oz. Rose's Lime Juice
1/2 cup of requested fruit
(Dash orange juice optional)
1 1/2 oz. sweet 'n' sour mix
Blend with ice
Garnish with appropriate fresh fruit
Note: Among the fruit choices include apple, apricot, banana, kiwi, melon, peach, pomegranate, raspberry, strawberry and watermelon.

If you have a piece of fruit on hand, and it hasn't officially spoiled, it can find a happy home in a margarita. Need convincing? Take a gander at the **Margarita de Fruta**,

NEON WATERMELON MARGARITA

House specialty glass, chilled
(Sugar rim optional)
1 1/4 oz. Sauza Silver Tequila
1 oz. Midori
1/2 oz. Rose's Triple Sec
1/2 cup frozen seedless watermelon chunks
3 oz. sweet 'n' sour mix
Blend with ice
Watermelon slice garnish

a recipe so expansive that it includes nearly every type of fruit described in the Encyclopedia Britannica. Blend up your favorite fruit and create a classic.

PINEAPPLE MARGARITA
a.k.a. PIÑARITA

Cocktail or house specialty glass, chilled
1 1/4 oz. Sauza Silver Tequila
3/4 oz. Rose's Triple Sec
1/2 cup pineapple chunks
1 1/2 oz. pineapple juice
Blend with ice
Fresh lime wedge garnish

PEAR MARGARITA
a.k.a. PEARITA

House specialty glass, chilled
(Salted rim optional)
1 1/2 oz. Sauza Silver Tequila
1/2 oz. Rose's Triple Sec
1 whole canned Bartlett pear
1/2 oz. Rose's Lime Juice
1 1/2 oz. sweet 'n' sour mix
Blend with ice
Fresh lime wheel garnish

RASPBERRY MARGARITA

House specialty glass, chilled
(Sugar rim optional)
  1 1/2 oz. Sauza Gold Tequila
  3/4 oz. Rose's Triple Sec
  1 1/2 oz. raspberry puree
  1 1/2 oz. orange juice
  1 1/2 oz. sweet 'n' sour mix
  Blend with ice
  Orange wheel and fresh lime wedge garnish

RED CACTUS MARGARITA

  House specialty glass, chilled
  (Sugar rim optional)
  1 1/4 oz. Sauza Gold Tequila
  1/2 oz. Rose's Triple Sec
  1/2 oz. Chambord
  1/2 oz. Rose's Lime Juice
  1/2 cup frozen raspberries
  1 1/2 oz. sweet 'n' sour mix
  Blend with ice
  Fresh lime wedge garnish

STRAWBERRY LOVER'S MARGARITA

House specialty glass, chilled
(Sugar rim optional)
1 oz. Sauza Silver Tequila
1 oz. Stolichnaya Strasberi Vodka
1/2 oz. Rose's Triple Sec
1/3 cup fresh or frozen strawberries
2 oz. sweet 'n' sour mix
Blend with ice
Strawberry garnish

WATERMELON MARGARITA

House specialty glass, chilled
(Sugar rim optional)
1 1/4 oz. Sauza Silver Tequila
3/4 oz. Rose's Triple Sec
1/2 cup frozen seedless watermelon chunks
3 oz. sweet 'n' sour mix
Blend with ice
Watermelon slice garnish

Don't ask us for suggestions on this page, our executive tasting team thoroughly enjoyed all of these specialties. The Red Cactus Margarita is universally appealing and a guaranteed "can't miss" crowd pleaser. Popular also is the Watermelon Margarita. Don't overlook the part about using frozen watermelon. The frozen fruit makes for a much more flavorful concoction.

BLENDED LAYERED/SWIRLED MARGARITAS

The better a drink looks, the better it seems to taste. If that's true, then the following margaritas must rate among the best tasting drinks ever. They may take a little more time to prepare, but we think soul-satisfying bliss is worth it.

MELTDOWN  MARGARITA

House specialty glass
(Salted rim optional)
1 1/4 oz. Sauza Silver Tequila
1/2 oz. Grand Marnier
1/2 oz. Rose's Lime Juice
1/2 oz. cranberry juice
1 1/2 oz. pureed raspberries
2 oz. sweet 'n' sour mix
Blend with ice
Float 3/4 oz. Chambord
Fresh lime wedge garnish

MIDNIGHT MADNESS MARGARITA

House specialty glass
(Salted rim optional)
Two blender canisters required
Step one/canister one
3/4 oz. Sauza Gold Tequila
3/4 oz. Blue Curaçao
1/2 oz. Rose's Lime Juice
1 1/2 oz. sweet 'n' sour mix
Blend with ice
Pour into glass
Step two/canister two
3/4 oz. Sauza Gold Tequila
3/4 oz. Chambord
1 oz. cranberry juice
1 oz. sweet 'n' sour mix
Blend with ice
Pour on top of first drink
Fresh lime wedge garnish

The **Midnight Madness Margarita** is an excellent example of a swirled specialty. The drink is made in two steps and requires two blender canisters. Blend each portion of the recipe with plenty of ice, then pour the second portion of the margarita on top of the first. The drink has two distinctively different looks and personalities. It makes for a striking presentation and a bona fide treat to slurp through a straw.

RASPBERRY TORTE MARGARITA

House specialty glass
 (Sugar rim optional)
  1 1/2 oz. Sauza Silver Tequila
  1/2 oz. Rose's Triple Sec
  2 oz. sweet 'n' sour mix
  Blend with ice
  Pour half of the drink into specialty glass;
  Add 2 oz. raspberry puree onto margarita in glass;
  Layer remainder of the margarita into glass creating layered effect
  with raspberry puree in middle;
  Orange wheel and lime wedge garnish

The divine Raspberry Torte Margarita and
Two-Toned Margarita are creations of El Charro's
resident margarita maestro, David Guerrero.
Two sips and you'll see why he's an institution in Tucson.

TWO-TONED MARGARITA

House specialty glass, ice
 (Salted rim optional)
 1 1/2 oz. Sauza Hornitos Reposado Tequila
 3/4 oz. Rose's Triple Sec
 1/2 oz. Rose's Lime Juice
 1 1/2 oz. orange juice
 2 oz. sweet 'n' sour mix
 Shake, strain, and fill glass 3/4 full;
 Pour remaining contents into blender with ice
 Add 1 oz. Midori
 Blend with ice
  Pour blended drink on top of iced margarita.
   Fresh lime wedge garnish
    Note: Chambord may be substituted for Midori to create a different
     flavor profile and presentation.

MARGARITA INFUSIONS

ICE BLUE MARGARITA INFUSION

Fill jar 1/3 full with lemon slices
Fill jar 1/6 full with lime slices
Fill jar 1/6 full with orange slices
1 liter Tequila
1 liter Midori
10 oz. Blue Curaçao

Wash, slice, and pit lemons, limes, and oranges. Add blue Curaçao, tequila, and Midori. Taste test after 2-3 days. Mix equal parts of infusion with sweet 'n' sour mix, shake and serve.

LEMONTREE MARGARITA INFUSION

Fill jar 1/4 full with lemons
Fill jar 1/4 full with limes
Fill jar 1/4 full with oranges
Add 2 liters Sauza Silver Tequila
Add 16 oz. Rose's Triple Sec
Add 6 oz. simple syrup

Wash, slice, and pit lemons, limes and oranges. Add simple syrup. Add triple sec and tequila. Taste test after 3-4 days. Mix equal parts of infusion with sweet 'n' sour mix, shake and serve.

SUMMER SHADES MARGARITA INFUSION

Fill jar 1/5 full with pineapples
Fill jar 1/5 full with cantaloupe
Fill jar 1/5 full with strawberries
Fill jar 1/5 full with peaches
1 liter Sauza Gold Tequila
1 liter Midori
10 oz. Blue Curaçao

Core, peel & slice pineapples into rings. Clean and cube cantaloupe. Wash and remove leaves from strawberries. Wash, cut and pit peaches. Add blue Curaçao, tequila and Midori. Taste test after 4-5 days. Mix equal parts of infusion with sweet 'n' sour mix, shake and serve.

Who ever thought of steeping a margarita with fresh fruit should be knighted. These concoctions are as delicious as they are clever. Mix a portion of the finished infusion with an equivalent amount of sweet 'n' sour, and *voila!*, an infused-margarita.

PUNCH MARGARITAS

MARGARITA PUNCH

Punch Bowl (256 oz.), quarter-full with ice
2 liters Sauza Gold Tequila
1.5 (750ml) bottles of chilled champagne
20 oz. Rose's Triple Sec
10 oz. Rose's Lime Juice
10 oz. orange juice
5 oz. fresh lime juice
18 oz. ginger ale
45 oz. sweet 'n' sour mix
Stir thoroughly
Orange, lemon, and lime wheels garnish

When a small gaggle of drinks is simply not enough, we give you margaritas fit for a punch bowl. They're guaranteed crowd-pleasers. Ladle some out and see.

MARGARITA SANGRIA

Pitcher (64 oz.), quarter-full with ice
20 oz. Dry red wine
12 oz. Sauza Gold Tequila
5 oz. Peach Schnapps
2 oz. Rose's Lime Juice
1 oz. grenadine
4 oz. orange juice
4 oz. sweet 'n' sour mix
Stir thoroughly
Orange, lemon, and lime wheels garnish

WINE MARGARITAS

CANTINA WINE MARGARITA

House specialty glass, ice
(Salted rim optional)
Build in glass
2 oz. Dry white wine
1 oz. Rose's Triple Sec
1/4 oz. Rose's Lime Juice
2 oz. sweet 'n' sour mix
Fill with club soda
Fresh lime wedge garnish

What's with the wine? Well, several of these recipes were created at restaurants with licenses that permit them to serve only beer and wine, the others feature wine as a flavoring agent. Whatever the initial reason behind their creation, these light, refreshing and flavorful concoctions are well worth sampling.

MIMOSARITA

Tulip champagne glass, chilled
1 1/2 oz. Sauza Gold Tequila
1/2 oz. Rose's Triple Sec
1/4 oz. Rose's Lime Juice
1 oz. orange juice
1 oz. sweet 'n' sour mix
Shake and strain
Fill with champagne
Orange twist garnish

SANGRIA 'RITA (F/G)

House specialty glass, ice
(Sugar rim optional)
1 oz. Sauza Silver Tequila
2 oz. Dry red wine
1/2 oz. Rose's Triple Sec
1/2 oz. Peach Schnapps
1/2 oz. Rose's Lime Juice
2 oz. sweet 'n' sour mix
Shake and strain
Float 2 each lemon, lime and orange wheels

VINTNER'S MARGARITA

Cocktail or house specialty glass, chilled
(Salted rim and ice optional)
3 oz. Dry white wine
1/2 oz. Rose's Triple Sec
1/2 oz. Rose's Lime Juice
1/2 oz. orange juice
2 oz. sweet 'n' sour mix
Shake and strain
Fresh lime wedge and orange wheel garnish

ZINFUL MARGARITA

Cocktail or house specialty glass, chilled
(Salted rim and ice optional)
1 1/4 oz. Sauza Gold Tequila
3 oz. White Zinfandel
1/2 oz. Chambord
1 oz. sweet 'n' sour mix
1/2 oz. Rose's Lime Juice
1 1/2 oz. orange juice
Shake and strain
Fresh lime wedge and orange wheel garnish

The Sangria is a national treasure in Spain, and with all due respect, the Sangria 'Rita is a marvelous adaptation of this timeless summer classic. Should you find yourself without tequila, yet have a serious hankering for a margarita, sip on the Vintner's Margarita. It's a refreshing placebo.

SHOOTER MARGARITAS

SHOOTAH 'RITA

Presentation shot glass
(Salted rim optional)
1 1/4 oz. Sauza Hornitos Tequila
1/2 oz. Rose's Triple Sec
1/4 oz. sweet 'n' sour mix
Juice from 1/4 fresh lime
Stir and strain
Fresh lime wedge garnish

ULTIMATE 'RITA SHOT

Presentation shot glass
(Salted rim optional)
3/4 oz. Sauza Tres Generaciones Tequila
3/4 oz. Cointreau®
1/4 oz. sweet 'n' sour mix
Juice from 1/4 fresh lime
Stir and strain
Fresh lime wedge garnish

The bottom line on Shooter Margaritas is that they're fun—plain and simple. Serve them in sherry glasses for an elegant presentation, or opt for a shot glass to get right to the point. Here's another idea...what about depth charging these beauties? Take a beer mug 3/4 full with a cold Mexican beer, a lager such as Corona or Tecate, and drop the shot glass with the drink into the beer. Then down the hatch. It's a great way to break up the week.

ALCOHOL-FREE MARGARITAS

VIRGIN MARGARITAS

(1) Cocktail or house specialty glass, ice (2)

2 oz. sweet 'n' sour mix (Salted rim optional) 1 oz. Rose's Triple Sec
1/2 oz. Rose's Triple Sec   2 oz. sweet 'n' sour mix
1 oz. orange juice   1/2 oz. Rose's Lime Juice
3/4 oz. Rose's Lime Juice   1/2 oz. orange juice
Shake and strain   Shake and strain
Fresh lime wedge garnish   Fresh lime wedge garnish

Not everyone is looking to socialize with alcohol, so why should they be left out of the fiesta? Don't they pay their taxes like the rest of us? Show them you care and shake up some of these delectable little numbers.

BEER MARGARITA

SAUZA MICHELADA

Pilsner or pint glass, ice
(Salted rim optional)
1 1/4 oz. Sauza Hornitos Tequila
1/2 oz. Rose's Lime Juice
6-7 oz. Corona Beer
Serve with bottle of Corona
Fresh lime wedge garnish

Alright, you caught us...the Michelada isn't really a margarita, but it's a darn refreshing twist on a longtime favorite from Mexico. Work up a thirst and see what we mean.

NON-TEQUILA MARGARITAS

BLUE MAESTRO GRAN MARGARITA

Cocktail or house specialty glass, chilled
(salted rim and ice optional)
3/4 oz. Mezcal del Maestro Añejo Reserva
3/4 oz. Citrus Mezcal del Maestro
1/2 oz. Grand Marnier
3/4 oz. Blue Curaçao
1/4 oz. Rose's Lime Juice
1 1/2 oz. sweet 'n' sour mix
Shake and strain
Fresh lime wedge garnish

If you want to be a stickler, and we can't imagine why you'd want to, these recipes are technically not margaritas. There's the minor detail that they don't contain tequila. They're such good tasting recipes, however, that leaving them out of the book seemed unthinkable.

CAPTAIN MARGARITA

Cocktail or house specialty glass, chilled
(salted rim and ice optional)
1 1/4 oz. Captain Morgan's Spiced Rum
1/2 oz. Rose's Triple Sec
1/2 oz. Rose's Lime Juice
2 oz. sweet 'n' sour mix
Shake and strain
Fresh lime wedge garnish

DEWAR'S MARGARITA

Cocktail or house specialty glass, chilled
(salted rim and ice optional)
1 1/4 oz. Dewar's Scotch
1/2 oz. Cointreau
1 1/2 oz. sweet 'n' sour mix
Shake and strain
Fresh lime wedge garnish

We're realistic. We know you're going to occasionally wander and entertain with spirits other than tequila. No need to feel guilty. Here's a few hand-picked candidates that are genuinely something extraordinary. Need help choosing? Try the French Classic Margarita. How can you possibly go wrong with Remy Martin Cognac and Cointreau®? Well, you can't!

FRENCH CLASSIC MARGARITA

Cocktail or house specialty glass, chilled
(Sugar rim and ice optional)
1 1/4 oz. Remy Martin VS Cognac
1/2 oz. Cointreau®
1 1/2 oz. sweet 'n' sour mix
Shake and strain
Fresh lemon wedge garnish

FRENCH/RUSSIAN MARGARITA

Cocktail or house specialty glass, chilled
(salted rim and ice optional)
1 1/4 oz. Stolichnaya Ohranj Vodka
1/2 oz. Grand Marnier
1/2 oz. Rose's Lime Juice
1/4 oz. orange juice
1 1/2 oz. sweet 'n' sour mix
Shake and strain
Orange twist garnish

JAMAICAN MARGARITA

Cocktail or house specialty glass, chilled
1 1/4 oz. Myers's Jamaican Rum
1/2 oz. Rose's Triple Sec
1/2 oz. Rose's Lime Juice
1/2 oz. orange juice
1 1/2 oz. sweet 'n' sour mix
Shake and strain
Fresh lime wedge garnish

KENTUCKY MARGARITA

Cocktail or house specialty glass, chilled
1 1/4 oz. Maker's Mark Bourbon
1/2 oz. Grand Marnier
1/4 oz. fresh lime juice
1 1/2 oz. sweet 'n' sour mix
Shake and strain
Fresh lime wedge garnish

Overlook the transgression and have some fun. After all, isn't imitation the sincerest form of flattery?

LIMONITA MARGARITA

Cocktail or house specialty glass, chilled
(Salted rim and ice optional)
1 1/4 oz. Stolichnaya Limonnaya Vodka
1/2 oz. Cointreau®
1/2 oz. Rose's Lime Juice
3/4 oz. cranberry juice
2 oz. sweet 'n' sour mix
Shake and strain
Fresh lemon wedge garnish

MALTA'S GRAPPARITA MARGARITA

Cocktail or house specialty glass, chilled
(Salted rim and ice optional)
1 1/4 oz. Grappa
3/4 oz. Rose's Triple Sec
1/2 oz. Rose's Lime Juice
1/2 oz. orange juice
2 oz. sweet 'n' sour mix
Shake and strain
Fresh lime wedge garnish

MOSCOW MARGARITA

Cocktail or house specialty glass, chilled
(Salted rim and ice optional)
1 1/2 oz. Smirnoff Vodka
1/2 oz. Rose's Triple Sec
1/2 oz. Rose's Lime Juice
2 oz. sweet 'n' sour mix
Shake and strain
Fresh lime wedge garnish

Rick Bayless is the chef-owner of the Chicago's fabulous Frontera Grill and the creative genius behind the specialty of the house, the Mezcal Margarita. This spicy, smoke-tinged concoction is a tour of Mexico in a glass. Grab your passport and jump on board.

MEZCAL MARGARITA

Cocktail or house specialty glass, chilled
(Salted rim and ice optional)
1 1/4 oz. Mezcal Añejo
1/2 oz. Brandy
2-3 dashes Peychaud bitters
1/2 oz. simple syrup
2 oz. sweet 'n' sour mix
Shake and strain
Fresh lime wedge garnish

MOUNT FUGI MARGARITA

Cocktail or house specialty glass, chilled
(Salted rim and ice optional)
2 oz. Sake
1/2 oz. Rose's Triple Sec
2 oz. sweet 'n' sour mix
Shake and strain
Lemon wheel garnish

RECIPES FROM COCINA CHARRO®

The margarita is a social animal that thrives surrounded by great food and drink. So what could possibly be better to include in a book that features such extraordinary margarita recipes than equally exceptional food recipes? It is equally fitting that these tequila-inspired recipes were created by Carlotta Flores, the 3rd generation chef-owner of El Charro Cafe, and more importantly, mother of Raymon Flores.

El Charro Cafe is a landmark around which Tucson has revolved since 1922. Its founder, Monica Flin, was a pioneering woman with an effusive personality who embraced life with both arms, a woman of gusto who loved good drink and great food. Monica drank her martinis out of tea cups and sipped her margaritas well chilled. Her Sonoran-style Mexican food drew critical and popular acclaim—then and now.

We invite you to sample a few of Carlotta's tequila-based creations—with a margarita or two, of course. Salud!

TEQUILA & AVOCADO CHUNKY SALSA

4 medium avocados, peeled, pitted and diced
4 medium firm tomatoes, diced or two pints
Cherry or orange teardrop tomatoes cut in halves
1 bunch green onions, finely chopped
6 fresh chile serranos minced
Salt to taste
1/3 cup lime juice
1/3 cup tequila
1 bunch finely chopped cilantro

Combine all ingredients in a non-reactive bowl, mixing with wooden spoon, cover with plastic wrap, cool in refrigerator for 1/2 hour. Serve as a dipping salsa, or as a condiment with your favorite beef or poultry entree.

TEQUILA MARINATED KABOBS

2 lbs. peeled and de-veined large shrimp,
or cubed chicken or beef
2 large green and red peppers cut into 1" pieces
1 white onion cut into 1" pieces
1 lb. large, clean mushrooms
2 Italian squashes cut into 1" pieces
Wooden skewers
Marinade
 1/2 cup tequila
 1/4 cup olive oil
 1/4 cup lime juice
 1/2 tsp. salt
 1/2 tsp. ground red pepper flakes

Refrigerate marinade mixture to blend. Soak wood skewers in water for at least 1/2 hour before assembling kabobs. Preheat broiler while assembling kabobs. Baste kabobs with marinade mixture (plan on 6-8 shrimp/chicken or beef cubes per kabob, alternate vegetables with the shrimp/chicken/beef. Above ingredients make 6 kabobs.)

Baste the kabobs with reserved marinade while grilling or broiling. Serve over white cilantro rice with lime wedges dipped in chili salt. To make chili salt, mix together 1/2 cup kosher salt, 1/4 cup red chili powder, and 1 tbs. ground garlic powder.

GUACAMOLE CON TEQUILA

6 large avocados, peeled, diced
1/4 cup diced white onions
1/3 cup tequila
1/4 cup finely diced cilantro
1/4 cup diced green onions
1 cup finely diced tomatoes
1 cup Mexican-style grated cheese, Cotija (salty) or Casero
4 minced chili serranos or jueritos
Salt to taste
Juice of 2 limes

Blend all of the above ingredients in a non-reactive bowl. Mash avocado pulp until thick and lumpy. Garnish with white Mexican-style Cotija or Casero grated cheese and serve with soft, warm tortillas, fresh cut vegetables, or your favorite totopos (chips).

TEQUILA MARINADE FOR POULTRY OR BEEF

1 oz. crushed chili flakes
1 oz. ground comino
2 tbs. Mexican leaf oregano
1 tbs. salt
1 oz. garlic powder
3/4 cup red wine vinegar
1/4 cup tequila
1 tbs. olive oil

Thoroughly mix all of the ingredients in a jar. Store in the refrigerator for 24 hours to allow the ingredients to marry. Shake the contents and pour over poultry or beef.

A few words of caution to avoid cross-contamination. Do not place poultry or beef in the same marinating dish. Discard the left over marinade remaining in the marinating dish; do not re-use! Do not mix marinade that has been used to marinate poultry or beef with unlike product(s).

Americans may be drinking less, but when they do drink, they're opting to drink the good stuff. The same mega-trend holds equally true for tequila and margaritas. For bar and restaurant operators, this bodes good news. Not only are premium tequilas hotter than a pistol, they're loaded with profit.

Promoting premium tequilas makes good financial sense. The top-shelf brands command higher retail prices and yield higher gross profits than less expensive tequilas. To illustrate the point, a margarita prepared with Sauza Silver Tequila has a raw cost of roughly $.61 and usually sells for about $3.25. The drink's cost percentage is therefore 18.8% ($.61/$3.25), and yields a gross profit of $2.64 ($3.25 - $.61).

A margarita made according to the same recipe using a premium tequila, such as Sauza Hornitos Reposado, sells at a higher cost percentage (20%), yet returns a higher gross profit of $3.60 (see inset). If the same drink were made with a super-premium tequila, such as Sauza Tres Generaciones Añejo, the cost percentage rises to 25.8%, but its gross profit increases to $4.45.

Margarita made with Sauza Silver Tequila

1 1/4 oz. Sauza Silver Tequila	=	$ .44
1/2 oz. triple sec	=	$ .06
1/2 oz. Rose's Lime Juice	=	$ .06
1 1/2 oz. sweetened 'n' sour	=	$ .05
Drink Cost		$ .61
$.61 cost/$3.25 sales price	=	18.8% cost
$3.25 sales price - $.61 cost	=	$2.64 gross profit

Margarita made with Sauza Hornitos Tequila

1 1/4 oz. Sauza Hornitos	=	$ .73
1/2 oz. triple sec	=	$ .06
1/2 oz. Rose's Lime Juice	=	$ .06
1 1/2 oz. sweetened 'n' sour	=	$ .05
Drink Cost		$ .90
$.90 cost/$4.50 sales price	=	20.0% cost
$4.50 sales price - $.90 cost	=	$3.60 gross profit

Margarita made with

Sauza Tres Generaciones Añejo

1 1/4 oz. Sauza Tres Generaciones	=	$1.38
1/2 oz. triple sec	=	$ .06
1/2 oz. Rose's Lime Juice	=	$ .06
1 1/2 oz. sweetened 'n' sour	=	$ .05
Drink Cost		$1.55
$1.55 cost/$6.00 sales price	=	25.8% cost
$6.00 sales price - $1.55 cost	=	$4.45 gross profit

So if you're more interested in your bar's bottom line than it's cost percentages, increasing your premium liquor sales should be a high priority.

SELECTING A TEQUILA INVENTORY

There are now nearly 200 labels of tequila being imported into the United States. With that many brands of tequila on the market, how do you determine which ones to stock? If you're just starting out in business, the best piece of advice is to be conservative, and start small. For most operations, opening with an adequate selection of the popular call and premium brands of tequila is sufficient. Be especially conservative when purchasing super-premium tequilas. For example, instead of initially carrying six or seven brands of añejos, stock two or three labels. As your business grows, your customers will begin requesting certain products, and your inventory will slowly expand.

For some beverage operators, stocking every brand of tequila is an integral aspect of their marketing concept. If a tequila is available, and potentially may hold some intrigue for a guest, the establishment will likely go ahead and stock it. The marketing concept here is, "If there's a possibility one of our guests might request a particular brand of tequila, we should have it."

Many bars and restaurants opt for a more conservative approach to marketing. They offer a somewhat limited selection of tequilas, each chosen as a capable representative of a specific style. So, for instance, instead of carrying every brand of 100% agave tequila, the establishment may choose to only promote the Sauza line. In this case the marketing concept is, "While we may not stock every available brand of tequila, what we do carry we serve with pride."

Still other operators may choose to carry a sufficiently broad selection of tequilas, one dominated by conventional brands without venturing into the more obscure labels. For example, the bar might carry three or four brands of blanco 100% agave tequilas, several labels of reposados, and a handful of añejos. All safe selections, offerings likely to meet most customers' requests. Here the marketing concept is, "Unless you throw us a curve, we likely carry it."

Each strategy has its merits. Conversely, each has its shortcomings. What is critically important is to ensure that the marketing strategy you chose is best suited for your establishment and clientele. Your understanding of the market will help you in answering two fundamental questions. One, how many brands of tequila should you stock for your establishment? And two, which brands of tequila should you carry in your inventory?

MARKETING 100% BLUE AGAVE TEQUILA

Their burgeoning popularity alone won't assure that these ultra-premium tequilas will attract a standing room only crowd at your bar. As with any high-ticket item, proper marketing will greatly assist your efforts to create customer brand-recognition.

The necessary first step is to educate your bartenders and servers about tequila. They should know what tequila is, what brands you carry, and what makes one brand different from another. The staff should also be well informed about what makes top-shelf tequilas so exceptional and why they command higher prices. Guests often inquire about what makes one brand better than another, and a concise, informative response is essential to selling super-premium brands.

Conduct horizontal-tastings for your staff and clientele so they can better experience first-hand the intriguing differences between the various brands. Ensure your staff is well informed about tequila, on what makes 100% blue agave tequilas so exceptional and why they're worth their higher price.

Encourage your clientele to sample short-portions of several different brands of tequila, so they can compare the attributes of each and determine their favorite styles. For instance, at El Charro Cafe in Tucson, the bar menu promotes five different "Tequila Tours." Guests are urged to be adventurous and conduct their own horizontal tastings, matching the character and personality of three, ideally paired tequilas. They are provided tasting portions (1/2 ounce) of each tequila. After the guests have had an opportunity to compare the three, the bartender discusses with them about their observations. Afterwards, guests will invariably purchase which ever tequila they preferred.

Suggestive sales techniques can also have a dramatic impact on guest appreciation and your bottom-line. For instance, when a guest orders a margarita, the server would be well-advised to respond, "Would you like a particular brand of tequila in your margarita?" Likewise, when someone orders a shot of tequila, the server should make specific recommendations, by saying "We highly recommend these brands. They taste great and they're reasonably priced. Would you like to try one in a shot?"

Suggestive sales isn't pushy or aggressive, it's a form of exceptional customer service. Isn't it true that a margarita made with a better grade of tequila is going to taste better? Shouldn't a server help guests make more informed decisions by making appropriate suggestions? Along the same lines, many people are accustomed to always ordering the same brand of tequila in a shot. Why not give them an opportunity to break out of the rut? Especially if the server's makes well-informed recommendations.

Equally important, make sure you provide support for your staff's efforts using standard marketing devices. Bar menus are a highly effective way to promote premium tequilas, specialty drinks and bar appetizers. Many operators also have success listing their top shelf spirits in a separate section on their wine menus.

Promote your specialty margaritas, as well as any food specials, on large wipe-off boards or chalk boards. They're inexpensive, effective marketing devices. Place them strategically around your establishment so there's never any question in anyone's mind what your daily specials are.

So whether you market the fine tequilas by Sauza, Herradura, or any and all of those mentioned in the book, stock up, because tequila is in hot demand. Now, and into the next millennium, the label you want your business saddled with is a "good tequila bar."

LOS TRES COMPADRES
TEQUILAS, LIQUEURS AND MIXES GLOSSARY

Absolut Vodkas ® — A line of premium pure grain vodkas produced since 1879 in Ahus, Sweden. The company produces an 80° and 100° version, as well as numerous flavored vodkas, including Citron (lemon-citrus), Peppar (pepper), and Kurant (currant).

Aguila Añejo Tequila ® — A 100% blue agave tequila produced at the El Viejito Distillery aged in oak barrels for over a year.

Blue Curaçao — An orange-flavored liqueur, slightly sweeter than Triple Sec, produced from the dried peels of oranges grown on the island of Curaçao.

Bonny Doon Framboise ® — A fortified wine (17% abv) infused with two varieties of Washington State raspberries. The raspberries are allowed to ferment briefly before unaged brandy is added, arresting the fermentation process.

Cabo Wabo Reposado Tequila ® — A 100% blue agave tequila produced at Agaveros Unidos de Amatitán in the highlands of Jalisco. It is aged between four and six months in both French and American oak barrels.

Calvados Apple Brandy — Named after the town of Calvados, in Normandy, France, it is distilled in pot stills from a mash of fermented cider apples. It is aged in oak casks for 3-10 years before blending and bottling.

Captain Morgan's Spiced Rum ® — An aromatic and flavorful blend of aged Puerto Rican rum and various spices, including clove, allspice and cinnamon.

Casa Noble Reposado Tequila ® — A 100% blue agave reposado tequila distilled at the La Cofridia Distillery in Jalisco. It is aged in oak barrels for three months.

Casta Tequila ® — A line of premium 100% blue agave tequilas produced at the Tequilera Newton e Hijos Distillery in Guadalajara. Casta tequilas are produced in four styles. The Casta Gusano Real Reposado is aged just short of a year in new white oak casks; Casta Oro Reposado is aged in new white oak casks and is blended with Casta Azul añejo; Casta Brava Reposado is aged six months to a year in used bourbon barrels; and Casta Weber Azul, a blend of añejo tequilas aged between one and five years.

Cazadores Reposado Tequila ® — Produced at the Cazadores Distillery located near the town of Arandas, Tequila Cazadores Reposado is aged in new oak barrels from Kentucky for a minimum of six months.

Centinela Tequila ® — A line of premium 100% blue agave tequilas produced in Arandas at the Centinela Distillery since 1894. Centinela tequilas are produced in four styles: a blanco, reposado, añejo, and a three-year old añejo.

Chambord Liqueur ® — A French framboise liqueur made from small black raspberries and various other fruits, herbs and honey.

Chinaco Tequila ® — A line of premium 100% blue agave tequilas made at La Gonzaleña Distillery. Chinaco tequilas are produced in three styles. Chinaco Blanco is bottled fresh directly out of the alembic still; Chinaco Reposado is aged in small oak casks between six months and a year; and Chinaco Añejo is aged for three-years in oak barrels.

Cointreau Liqueur ® — Cointreau®, the superpremium French liqueur, is blended from the world's most exotic and exclusive orange peels. This renowned and distinguished liqueur was created in 1849 by Edouard Cointreau in the historic city of Angers, on the banks of the river Maine.

In the mid-1800s, Edouard Cointreau began to notice that traditional opaque liqueurs packaged in ornate bottles were losing popularity. He set out to create a dramatically different type of spirit—a clear liqueur with a pronounced taste of oranges, packaged in a distinctive and elegant way.

The recipe for Cointreau® has remained a secret and passed down from generation to generation. Today only five members of the Cointreau family know the secret recipe. It blends sweet and bitter orange peels, alcohol and water, all of which are distilled to perfection according to the original standards Edouard Cointreau established in 1849. Sugar is the last ingredient that is added to the finished product.

The sweet and bitter orange peels, the essence of Cointreau®, are carefully grown and meticulously selected. The sweet orange peels originate from Santa Barbara, Spain, and Brazil. Four major varieties are used: the Comuna, Cadanera, Pera and the Salustiana. The bitter peels are cultivated in Cointreau®'s plantations in Haiti and come from the highly regarded Bigarade orange.

Knowing that the fruit could not withstand the rigors of a long ocean voyage from the Caribbean and the tropics, Edouard decided to use only the dried peels of the fruit. He discovered the best way to bring out their delicious aroma and flavor was to steep them in fine brandy.

Cointreau®'s master distiller guides the transmutation of the raw materials. After selection, the shredded sweet and bitter peels are placed into oak barrels, filled with brandy and aged for three to eighteen months. When the infusions have reached their peak flavor, the casks are drained.

The various varieties of orange spirits are blended together until the balanced flavor profile has been achieved. The infusions are then distilled twice in red copper alembic stills. The distillery has nineteen stills, each designed specifically to produce Cointreau®. The other ingredients—alcohol, water, and sugar—are selected for their absolute purity and neutrality of taste.

The finished liqueur is taste-tested by a team of esteemed professionals to ensure that it is faithful in every way to Edouard Cointreau's original demands.

Corralejo Reposado Tequila ® — A 100% blue agave reposado tequila produced at the Tequilera Corralejo Distillery in Guanajuato. It is aged eleven months in French Limousin oak barrels.

Creme de Banana — A banana-flavored cordial.

Curaçao — see Blue Curaçao

Damiana Liqueur ® — After a fifty year hiatus, Damiana Liqueur is again available in the United States. It is made from an aromatic flower indigenous to the mountains of Jalisco. It is a revered plant in Mexico and is purported to be an aphrodisiac.

Dewar's Scotch Whisky ® — Established in the 1860's, John Dewar is credited with bottling the first Scotch whiskey. The company produces two blended Scotch whiskies: White Label and a 12-year-old super premium, Dewar's 12.

Di Saronno Amaretto ® — The original and best known brand of amaretto, Di Saronno is a reddish-brown aromatic liqueur, with a sweet almond flavor. It is made from a 400-year old recipe of neutral spirits, herbs, and apricot pits.

Don Eduardo Tequila ® — A line of premium 100% blue agave tequilas produced in Jalisco at the Tequila Orendain Distillery. Named for Orendain's master tequilero, Don Eduardo Gonzalez, the tequila is produced in two styles; a silver and a two-year old añejo.

Don Julio Tequila ® — A line of premium 100% blue agave tequilas made at the Tequila Tres Magueyes distillery by tequilero Don Julio Gonzalez. The distillery has currently released for export two styles of Don Julio Tequila, a blanco and an añejo.

El Conquistador Tequila ® — A line of premium 100% blue agave tequilas produced at the Agroindustrias Guadalajara Distillery. El Conquistador Tequilas are produced in three styles: unaged El Conquistador Blanco; El Conquistador Reposado is aged a minimum of seven-months in oak barrels; and El Conquistador Añejo is aged over a year in French oak barrels.

El Jimador Reposado Tequila ® — A 100% blue agave reposado produced by Herradura. It is aged between two and three months in oak barrels.

El Tesoro de Don Felipe Tequila ® — A line of premium 100% blue agave tequilas made at La Alteña Distillery in the Los Altos mountains. El Tesoro Tequilas are produced in four styles. El Tesoro Silver Tequila is bottled directly out of the alembic still; El Tesoro Reposado Tequila is aged in small oak casks between two months and one year; and El Tesoro Añejo is aged for two to three years in used bourbon barrels. El Tesoro Paradiso Añejo is an innovative style of tequila. It is a five-year-old añejo, crafted from a blend of El Tesoro Silver and El Tesoro Añejo. Paradiso Añejo is then aged further in French oak barrels previously used to age A. de Fussigny Cognac.

Frangelico Liqueur ® — An Italian liqueur made from a 300-year-old recipe of wild hazelnuts, berries and spices.

Gran Centenario Tequila ® — A line of premium 100% blue agave tequilas made at the Los Camachines Distillery in Los Altos de Jalisco. Gran Centenario Tequilas are produced in three styles; a blanco, reposado, and Gran Centenario Añejo, which is aged for up to 18 months in charred, white-oak casks.

Grand Marnier Liqueur ® — A French liqueur produced by the Lapostolle family since 1827. Its flavor and bouquet are derived from a blend of wild bitter oranges and cognac.

Grappa — A colorless, unaged Italian brandy distilled from grape pomace, the remnants of the wine-making process. Grappa is technically an Eau de Vie Marc.

Herradura Tequila ® — A line of premium 100% blue agave tequilas made at the Herradura Distillery in Amatitan. Herradura was the first 100% blue agave tequila available in the United States. It is produced in five styles: a silver; gold; Herradura Reposado is aged between two and eleven months in oak barrels; and Herradura Añejo is barrel aged between one to four years. Herradura Selección Suprema Tequila was issued in 1996 to commemorate the company's 125th anniversary. Selección Suprema is a superpremium tequila crafted from a select blend of five-year old tequilas aged in white oak barrels.

Hussong's Reposado ® — A 100% blue agave reposado tequila produced at the El Viejito Distillery. It aged between three and six months in oak barrels.

Jose Cuervo Tequila ® — A line of premium tequilas, both mixtos and 100% blue agave, made at the La Rojeña Distillery in the town of Tequila. Jose Cuervo is the largest distiller of tequila, as well as the oldest, the company having received its grant from the King of Spain in 1795. Jose Cuervo produces three labels of mixto tequilas: a silver; Especial, a joven abocado tequila; and 1800.

Jose Cuervo also produces four labels of 100% blue agave tequila: Tradicional, a reposado aged in white oak casks for 6 months; Reserva Antigua 1800 Añejo, aged for a year in small, charred French oak casks; and Jose Cuervo Añejo, aged for more than a year in American white oak barrels. Jose Cuervo Reserva de la Familia was released to commemorate their 200th anniversary. Reserva de la Familia de Jose Cuervo is a superpremium añejo aged three years in small oak casks.

La Cava de Don Agustin Tequila ® — A premium 100% blue agave reposado made at the La Arandina Distillery in the Highlands of Jalisco. La Cava de Don Agustin is aged for 11 months in small, American oak barrels.

Lapis Tequila ® — A line of premium 100% agave tequilas produced at the La Tequileña Distillery in the town of Tequila. Originally founded in 1967, the company was purchased in 1990 by Enrique Fonseca, the largest agave farmer in Jalisco. Lapis Tequilas are produced in two styles, a silver called Platinum and a two-year old añejo. Lapis Tequila was originally marketed in the United States as Lapiz.

Licor 43 (Cuarenta y Tres) ® — A Spanish liqueur made from vanilla, citrus, milk, and 43 different herbs.

Lillet ® — A semi-dry, fortified aperitif wine (18% abv) with the subtle flavor of oranges, herbs and quinine. Lillet has been produced in France since 1872 in two versions: Blonde (drier and made with white wine) and Rouge (sweeter and made with red wine).

Luna Azul Tequila ® — A line of 100% blue agave tequilas made at Rancho La Laja Distillery located near Zapotlanejo. Luna Azul tequilas are produced in two styles: a reposado aged eleven months in used Kentucky bourbon barrels; and a two-year old añejo.

Makers Mark Kentucky Bourbon ® — A straight Kentucky bourbon whiskey made since 1889 in Loretto, Kentucky.

Malibu Rum ® — A liqueur made from Jamaican light rum and coconut.

Mezcal del Maestro ® — A line of premium 100% agave mezcals double distilled in small batches in Oaxaca, Mexico. There are three styles of Mezcal Del Maestro: a citrus-infused mezcal; a reposado aged in oak barrels a minimum of three months; and the Añejo Reserva, a single barrel mezcal aged in charred, American white oak barrels for two years.

Midori Liqueur ® — A Japanese honeydew liqueur produced by Suntory.

Myers's Jamaican Rum ® — Produced in Kingstown, Jamaica, since 1879, Myers's is best known for their flavorful and full-bodied Original Dark Rum.

1921 Tequila ® — A line of premium 100% blue agave tequilas produced at the Agave Tequilana Productores y Comercialzadores Distillery located in the highlands of Jalisco. There are three styles of 1921 Tequila: a blanco, reposado, and an añejo.

Patrón Tequila ® — A line of premium 100% blue agave tequilas produced at Tequila Siete Leguas in the highlands of Jalisco. There are three styles of the popular Tequila Patrón: a blanco, a reposado aged in oak barrels for a minimum of six months, and the two-year old añejo.

Porfidio Tequila ® — A line of premium 100% blue agave tequilas made at several different distilleries. There are six styles of

Porfidio Tequila: a silver; a triple-distilled plata; a reposado aged in oak barrels between six and eleven months; an añejo aged in small oak casks for two years; and the single barrel añejo. Barrique de Ponciano is a 100% blue agave añejo, aged for two years in new, small (100-liter) French Limousin oak barrels.

Presidente Brandy ® — A light, Mexican brandy distilled from Mission grapes.

Remy Martin Cognac ® — Founded in 1724, Remy Martin exclusively features well-aged Grande and Petite brandies with a pronounced fruit and spicy character. Remy Martin's top-end cognacs—the XO Special (20-25 year), Extra Perfection (30 year), and the famed Louis XIII Grande Champagne (50 years)—rank among the finest and most recognized brandies.

Reserva Del Dueño Añejo ® — A premium 100% blue agave añejo tequila produced at the Fabrica de Aguardiente de Agave la Mexicana outside of Arandas. It is aged for between one and two years in American oak bourbon casks and bottled at 83.4 proof.

Rose's Lime Juice ® — Rose's Lime Juice is a storied product with a rich adventure-laced heritage. It has its origins in the tall sailing ships that navigated the warm waters of the West Indies.

Lauchlin Rose (1829-1885) was a descendent of a prominent Scottish shipbuilding family. In 1865, he founded the L. Rose & Company in Leith, Edinburgh. Her Majesty's Navy needed lime juice to preserve the Empire. Sailors needed the ascorbic acid in fruits such as limes to ward off the debilitating effects of scurvy. Rose's firm provided the navy with life-preserving lime juice.

At first the juice was preserved by adding 15% rum. In 1867, Lauchlin Rose developed and patented a process for preserving fresh lime juice without the use of alcohol. That same year, the Merchant Shipping Act was passed requiring all Royal Navy and Merchant vessels to dispense a daily ration of lime juice. It was this law that brought about the use of the slang name "Limeys" for British sailors, as well as generated widespread acclaim for Rose's Lime Juice.

The firm soon relocated to England from Scotland. In 1895, L. Rose & Company bought huge land holdings at the Bath Estate on Dominica in the Caribbean's Windward Islands. Exports of Rose's Lime Juice continued to increase, and in 1901 the first shipment was received in the United States.

In 1916, the company expanded its lime plantations to Africa, locating in the fertile region of the Gold Coast, now known as Ghana. During World War II the L. Rose & Company relocated to its present location in St. Albans, northwest of London. Rose's Lime Juice continues as the best selling lime juice in the world.

In 1998, the company identified the growing trend toward using non-alcoholic products in drink making and introduced Rose's Triple Sec, a full-flavored, alcohol-free cordial. It is ideally suited for use in scores of cocktails, including margaritas, kamikazes, Long Island Iced Teas, and cosmopolitans.

Sake — A colorless brewed alcoholic beverage made from rice. It is technically and legally defined as rice beer.

Sauza Tequila ® — (see pages 11-19 for more information on Sauza tequila) A line of premium tequilas, both mixtos and 100% blue agave, made at the La Perseverancia Distillery in the town of Tequila. Tequila Sauza is the second largest distiller of tequila, and the fastest growing spirit brand in the world. Now the best selling tequila in Mexico, Tequila Sauza produces three premiere brands of mixto tequila: **Sauza Blanco**, a silver tequila; **Sauza Extra Gold**, a joven abocado tequila; and **Sauza Conmemorativo**, an añejo aged for two years in small, white American oak barrels called barricas de roble.

Sauza also produces four labels of 100% blue agave tequila: **Sauza Hornitos Reposado**, aged in wood for four to six months; **Sauza Galardon Gran Reposado**, produced in small batches and aged in white-oak casks up to one-year; and **Sauza Tres Generaciones**, an añejo aged a minimum of three years in 180-liter white oak barrels. Superpremium **Sauza Triada Añejo** is double distilled from the first pressing of the agaves. Sauza Triada is also the product of a singular, two-stage aging process. It is first aged as a reposado in large oak vats. After roughly six months, the tequila is transferred to 180-liter, oak bourbon barrels. Triada Añejo is left in the barrel for over three years.

Smirnoff Vodka ® — An American, charcoal-filtered vodka made from corn by Heublein in Connecticut since the 1934. It is produced according to a recipe first devised by Piotr Smirnoff in 1818.

Stolichnaya Vodka ® — Pure grain vodkas produced in Moscow, among other places, at the Cristall Distillery, Russia's oldest and most renowned distillery. The company produces an 80° and 100° version, as well as numerous flavored vodkas, including Pertsovka (pepper), Ohranj (orange), Okhotnichya (herb and honey), Limonnaya (lemon), Kafya (coffee), Vanil (vanilla), Zinamon (cinnamon), Razberi (raspberry), Strasberi (strawberry), and Persik (peach). The company's flagship is Stolichnaya Gold, a superpremium small batch vodka quadruple distilled at the Liviz Distillery in St. Petersburg from winter wheat and soft, glacial water.

Tia Maria Liqueur ® — A liqueur produced from a blend of Blue Mountain coffee beans, chocolate and Jamaican rum since the late 1700s.

Treinta y Treinta Tequila ® — A line of 100% blue agave tequilas made at the Agroindustria Distillery in the Highlands of Jalisco. The Treinta y Treinta (30-30) tequilas are produced in three styles; a blanco, reposado and añejo.

Tres Mujeres Reposado ® — A 100% blue agave reposado tequila produced at the J. Jesus Partida Melendez Distillery outside of Amatitan. The reposado is aged between three and six months.

Triple Sec — A clear, triple-distilled orange-flavored liqueur made from the peels of bitter Curaçao oranges. Although sometimes, referred to as "White Curaçao," triple sec is drier than Curaçaos.

Tuaca Liqueur ® — A complex, semi-sweet Italian liqueur made from herbs, fruit peels.

Zafarrancho Tequila ® — A line of premium 100% blue agave tequilas made at Rancho La Laja Distillery located near Zapotlanejo. Zafarrancho tequilas are produced in four styles: a silver, gold, a joven abocado tequila; a reposado aged a minimum of four months in oak barrels previously used to age bourbon; and an añejo aged in small oak casks for between 18 months and two years.

MARGARITA RECIPE INDEX

Looking for a particular recipe? We thought you might, so here are all 125 margarita recipes listed alphabetically, including their a.k.a.'s, and a notation of which category each recipe can be found.

Milliliter (ml) = 0.0338 oz = 0.204 tsp
Teaspoon (tsp) = 0.166 oz = 0.33 Tbs = 4.927ml
Tablespoon (Tbs) = 3 tsp = 0.5 oz = 14.78ml
Ounce (US) = 8 tsp. = 29.57ml
Ounce (UK) = 1.0408 US oz = 30.78ml
Jigger = 1.5 oz = 44.35ml
Cup = 8 oz = 236.56ml
Pint = 16 oz = 473.12ml = .473 l
Quart (qt) = 32 oz = 946.24ml = .946 l
Liter (l) = 0.9463 qt = 33.8146 oz = 1000ml = 1 l
Gallon (gal) = 4 qt = 128 oz = 3.786 l = 3784.96ml 3.784 l

Wine & Spirits Bottle Capacities
(Ascending Capacity)
Champagne & Wine Split = 1/4 bottle = 6.35 oz = 187.5ml
Half-Bottle Wine (Fillet) = 12.7 oz = 375ml
Imperial Wine = 19.5 oz = 576.6ml
Alsatian Wine = 24.34 oz = 720ml
Wine Bottle = 25.4 oz = 750ml
US Fifth (Spirits) = 25.6 oz = 756.9ml
Magnum = 2 wine bottles = 50.7 oz = 1.5 l
Flagan = 2 qt. = 64 oz = 1.893 l
Jeroboam = 4 wine bottles = 101.4 oz = 3 l
Rehoboam = 6 wine bottles = 152.1 oz = 4.5 l
Imperial Gallon = 1.2 US gal. = 153.7 oz = 4.545 l
Bordelaise = 6.66 wine bottles = 169 oz = 5 l
Methuselah = 8 wine bottles = 202.8 oz = 5.997 l
Salamanzar = 12 wine bottles = 304.2 oz = 8.995 l
Balthazar = 16 wine bottles = 405.6 oz 12.02 l
Nebuchadnezzar = 20 wine bottles = 507.1 oz = 14.99 l

Weights
Gram (g) = 0.035 oz
Ounce (oz) = 28 g
Pound (lb) = 16 oz. = 448 g
Kilogram (kg) = 1000 g = 2.2046 lbs

RESOURCES

Following is a list of the companies, products, and people that made ¡Toma! Margaritas! a success. We whole-heartedly recommend that you contact these quality individuals and companies concerning their products and services.

If there is a product mentioned in the book that you are having trouble finding which is not listed, you may contact the publisher for further information.

Domecq Importers Inc.
A Division of Allied Domecq
Spirits and Wine
355 Riverside Ave.
Westport, CT 06880
203.221.5400
     Products: Sauza Blanco Tequila, Sauza Extra Gold Tequila, Sauza Conmemorativo Añejo Tequila, Sauza Hornitos Reposado 100% Agave Tequila, Sauza Galardon Gran Reposado Tequila, Sauza Tres Generaciones Añejo 100% Agave Tequila, Sauza Triada Añejo 100% Agave Tequila

Remy Amerique
1350 Avenue of the Americas
New York, NY 10019
212.399.4200
     Cointreau® Liqueur

Motts North America
6 High Ridge Park
P.O. Box 3800
Stamford, CT 06905
203.968.7812
     Roses Lime Juice
     Roses Non-alcoholic Triple Sec

Blendex Company
11208 Electron Drive
Louisville, KY 40299
502.267.1003
     colored salt & sugar

Twang
800 Buena Vista, Bldg. 2, Suite 200
San Antonio, TX 78207
210.226.7008
     flavored salt

Franco's Cocktail Mixes
121 S.W. 5th Court
Pompano Beach, FL 33060
     colored salt

Orion Trading
1927 E. 19th St.
Tucson, AZ 85719
520.622.6588
Contact: Jim de Girolamo
     Importer of Authentic mouth-blown and hand-formed Mexican glassware made from recycled pop bottles. This artistic glassware(as seen on the cover) is redefining elegance. A purveyer for world-class resorts and retail outlets nationwide.

Design
 • Miguel Castillo ~ CastleBay
Tucson, AZ ~ cbsgd@aol.com
or contact publisher for information
     (book design and collaboration
     on cover design)

Photography
 • Maria Cecilia Boyed Photography
Tucson, AZ
contact publisher for information
     (cover photography)
 • Eric Hinote Photography
contact publisher for information
     (product photography)

Raymon Flores
Chonita Foods®/Cocina Charro®
847 E. 18th St.
Tucson, AZ 85719
     800.678.3689/fax.520.884.0878
     (food recipes)

Founded in 1987 by Robert Plotkin, BarMedia has created a line of products for the professional beverage operator as well as the home entertainer. From drink recipe guides to cost control management texts, quality products at reasonable prices, each with an unconditional money-back guarantee. For a complete list of all of our products call 1.800.421.7179, on-line: www.barmedia.com, or email a request for more info: barinfo@barmedia.com.

Robert Plotkin, founder, BarMedia, has a mission

AMERICA'S FAVORITE DRINK RECIPE GUIDE

It's America's favorite drink recipe guide in an easy to use spiral binding. Filled with all of the popular drinks and all the classics, plus huge sections on the megatrend drinks as well. Martinis and Manhattans, Margaritas, Infusions, Bloody Marys, shooters and more. It's the only guide with a thorough index of drinks grouped by type and main ingredient. Responsibly portioned, taste-tested for quality, unconditionally guaranteed. **The Bartender's Companion Complete Drink Recipe Guide** • by Robert Plotkin • 169 pages • 6" x 9" • $17.95

THE SECRETS TO MAKING AUTHENTIC, SONORAN MEXICAN DISHES

You may have never enjoyed exciting fresh Mexican food like this. In her beautifully illustrated cookbook, chef Carlotta Flores, (Ray's Mom) shares original recipes, her colorful family history and her love for this cuisine — unique to Tucson, Arizona, and the surrounding Sonoran desert. These prized family recipes are easy to prepare and will guarantee your reputation as a wonderful cook. **El Charro Café, The Tastes and Traditions of Tucson** • by Carlotta Flores 136 pages • 7.75" x 11.5" • $24.95 • hardcover

YOUR BLUEPRINT FOR BEVERAGE MARKETING

Create your own blueprint for building better drinks, and learn the creative, profitable twists behind today's most successful Martinis, Manhattans, Infusions, Margaritas, and classic cocktails. Increase your bar's revenues with a straight-forward, step-by step program. Learn about the megatrends that are affecting your business, and discover how to use the boom in superpremium spirits to increase your profits. This will likely become the most important investment you make in your beverage operation. **Increasing Bar Sales, Creative Twists to Bigger Profits** • by Robert Plotkin • 206 pages • 6" x 9" • $24.95

AMERICA'S FAVORITE BEVERAGE MANAGEMENT NEWSLETTER

Published by industry expert and bartending guru Robert Plotkin, it's the best in beverage management — current trends and management tips, seasonal recipes and product reviews, as well as market trends, drink trends, tricks of the trade, promotion ideas and bar trivia. A must have for the successful on-premise operator and manager. Get six information-packed issues per year. **The American Mixologist newsletter** • 8 pages • 8.5" x 11" • $35 • overseas add $20.00